HARVEY HOUSES
of ARIZONA

HARVEY HOUSES
of ARIZONA

Historic Hospitality from Winslow to the Grand Canyon

ROSA WALSTON LATIMER

THE
History
PRESS

Published by The History Press
Charleston, SC
www.historypress.net

Front cover, top: Harvey Girls at the lunch counter of the Harvey House in Winslow, Arizona, circa 1910. *Courtesy of Arizona State Library, Archives and Public Records, History and Archives Division, Phoenix, No. 98-9814; bottom*: La Posada in Winslow, Arizona, was the last Fred Harvey hotel built. It opened in 1930, closed in 1957 and, after restoration, is now once again welcoming guests. *Courtesy of Tom Taylor.*

Back cover, left: The curio shop at the Escalante offered a large display of Native American arts and crafts for sale. *Courtesy of Tom Taylor; right*: Harvey Girls with manager W.E. Belding (*center*) at the Harvey House in Winslow, Arizona, circa 1920. Olive Van Zoast, who later became a rancher known as Cecil Creswell, is third from right. *Courtesy of Old Trails Museum and Winslow Historical Society.*

First published 2019

Manufactured in the United States

ISBN 9781625858566

Library of Congress Control Number: 2018966258

Notice: The information in this book is true and complete to the best of our knowledge. It is offered without guarantee on the part of the author or The History Press. The author and The History Press disclaim all liability in connection with the use of this book.

Dedicated to my sweet daughter,
Dr. Lara A. Latimer
She is always there for me in all ways.

Fond memories and love for "His Happiness,"
Dr. James Bell
Your unfailing love and kindness are with me still.

CONTENTS

CONTENTS

ACKNOWLEDGEMENTS

*S*ince I began the work of preserving the story of Fred Harvey, Harvey Girls and Harvey Guys, there have been individuals who have remained loyal to my projects and have consistently offered assistance with information and images. I always know these folks are just a text or message away, and I am very thankful for their valuable support: Michael McMillan, Everet Apodaca, Heather Paxton and Melissa Morrow.

My special thanks to Tom Taylor for his valuable contribution to this book as well as the outstanding tour of all things Fred Harvey (and Louis Curtiss) in Kansas City. A day I'll never forget, Tom!

Thank you, Allan Affeldt, for your support and for your dedication to the Fred Harvey history. Because of your incredible investment of time, resources and energy to preserve La Posada (Winslow, Arizona) and the Castaneda (Las Vegas, New Mexico), the tradition of Fred Harvey hospitality lives on!

Many thanks to Danyelle Gentry Peterson and Beau Gentry for sharing images from their father's impressive Fred Harvey Memorabilia Collection. I didn't know Skip Gentry, but from all accounts, he was a terrific guy who loved all things Fred Harvey.

A sincere "thank you" to Ann-Mary Lutzick, Old Trails Museum; Matthew Smith, National Park Service; Katherine Lauster, Chino Valley Historical Society; and Brenda Thowe for your help with research.

My entire Fred Harvey experience would not have been quite as much fun without the camaraderie of dear friends Kathy Beach, Meredith Edwards, Kathy Hendrickson, Jim and Kathy Weir and John Valdes. Thanks for the good times!

INTRODUCTION

The week I graduated from high school, I received a large envelope with an out-of-state postmark. The name on the return address was "Balmanno." This name had never been spoken in our house, but before I was adopted, it was my family name. My adoptive mother laid the unopened envelope on my desk, silently giving permission for me to read the contents.

The long letter inside, from my biological uncle, provided a wonderful family connection for me. In handwriting almost identical to my own, Uncle Bill told stories about every branch of our family tree. The paragraphs about my grandparents particularly captured my attention.

Gertrude Elizabeth McCormick met my grandfather William Alexander Balmanno in 1913 while she was working as a Harvey Girl in New Mexico. When William was twelve years old, he left his family on the island of Mauritius in the Indian Ocean to work on whaling ships. At the age of twenty-nine, he and a friend quit their whaling days in Vera Cruz, Mexico, and decided to walk to California. On the way, in Rincon, New Mexico, William took a job with the Santa Fe Railroad to earn money to finish his trip.

My grandmother, an orphan who had finished nursing school in Philadelphia, wanted to go to Alaska (looking for adventure, I suppose). She reasoned that working as a Harvey Girl would be a good start, as it afforded the opportunity to transfer to different locations all the way to California. Her first assignment was at the lunch counter in the Harvey House in

Rincon, where she met William. They married three months later and lived the rest of their lives in the Southwest.

My uncle seemed quite proud of his mother's ties to the Harvey Houses built along the Santa Fe Railroad. He also assumed that I knew the story of the Harvey Girls and their strong influence on the settling of the West. I had no idea what he was talking about, but I wanted to know more about these Harvey Girls.

Lesley Poling-Kempes, author of *The Harvey Girls*, published in 1989, describes her book as emphasizing the historical importance of ordinary people. I'm using Lesley's words here to encourage anyone reading this book to recognize the importance of your family history, the story of your hometown—stories of ordinary people—and to begin to preserve that history.

Writing a series of books on Harvey Houses is my way of paying tribute to my grandmother, a woman somewhat mysterious to me, as I last saw her when I was two years old. This is also my way of recognizing the many young women who answered Fred Harvey's advertisements for "educated women of good character" to work in Harvey Houses, many of whom headed west at a time when careers for young women were limited to teacher or nurse—a time when working as a waitress was not considered a respectable occupation for young, single women.

It is generally stated that over 100,000 women worked as Harvey Girls beginning in the late nineteenth century and continuing until the late 1940s, when most of the Harvey restaurants had closed.

When Fred Harvey handpicked waitresses, dressed them in proper, starched uniforms and sent them out to feed the traveling public, I am not sure he realized how Harvey Girls would change the course of history. Many were the first women to venture more than walking distance from their hometowns. Others had traveled extensively and recognized the prospect of adventure in the West. Surely, the Harvey Girl hopefuls were all keenly aware that working in a remote place where few women lived would provide many opportunities for meeting a prospective husband.

Harvey Girl Emily Hahn may have best explained why so many answered Harvey's call with the title of her book: *Nobody Said Not to Go*. Emily, who says she traveled across the United States in the 1920s dressed as a boy before she became a Harvey Girl, had many adventures during her lifetime, all because "nobody said not to go."

I can imagine there were many times when a young woman's mother, under the stern gaze of a protective father, would not say "Go!" but also did not say "Don't go." Perhaps the older woman had yearned for adventure at

Winslow Harvey Girl Jenny Sterling is wearing a nontraditional uniform featuring a black apron adorned with colorful applique and trim. *Courtesy of Old Trails Museum and Winslow Historical Society.*

a young age and realized this chance to be a Harvey Girl offered hope for a better life for her daughter. Even if parents encouraged a daughter to seize the opportunity, their attitude may have changed when, after six months or a year, they received a letter announcing marriage to a Santa Fe brakeman or a local rancher.

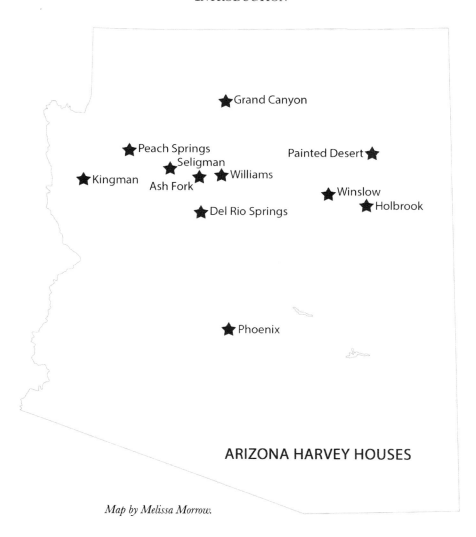

Map by Melissa Morrow.

Harvey Girls worked hard, had some fun and made Fred Harvey proud. Through the years, their income usually exceeded what was paid in other professions available to young women. Many sent money home to help their families through the Depression years or paid for a college education, which led to successful careers beyond the Harvey House dining room.

Over twenty years ago, Arizona artist Tina Mion and her husband, Allan Affeldt, purchased and restored the last Fred Harvey hotel, La Posada, which was built in 1930 in Winslow, Arizona. (The couple is now restoring another Harvey hotel, the Castaneda, in Las Vegas, New Mexico.) When the couple moved to Winslow, they became close friends with former Harvey Girls who still lived in the area. Mion produced a painting titled *The Last Harvey Girl* depicting two of these long-retired women: Ruby Gardner McHood and Dorothy Hunt. In the painting, Ruby is wearing a white blouse, a black bow tie and a skirt adorned with colorful applique and trim. This style (or some version) of Harvey Girl uniform was typically worn in tourist-savvy Harvey Houses in New Mexico, Arizona and California. As Dorothy sits in the shadows, hands folded in her lap, Ruby stands, leaning on a walking cane, holding a cup of tea. She appears to be offering the tea to the viewer.

Dorothy Bailey Hunt was an experienced Harvey Girl on staff at Harvey restaurants in the Grand Canyon and La Posada in Winslow for almost fifteen years. Ruby Gardner McHood worked at La Posada for two years before leaving to marry Winslow resident Mac McHood.

In a statement about the painting, the artist said, "Only a handful of Harvey Girls remain. One day soon, someone will be handed a cup of tea or coffee by the last Harvey Girl and, in an anonymous kitchen or living room, an era will silently pass." The artist intends for the viewer to be the honored recipient of the passing of this era.

The Harvey Girl era has indeed slipped away. This book is a celebration of the experiences and accomplishments of these adventuresome women and a reminder of how Fred Harvey and his Harvey Girls changed the culture of railroad towns along the Atchison, Topeka & Santa Fe Railway. It is my hope that this book will help carve a broader niche in Arizona history for these spirited, hardworking women.

1

THE HARVEY STANDARD
OF EXCELLENCE

Fred Harvey's narrative in the United States began when the Englishman emigrated in 1850 at the age of fifteen. Harvey learned the restaurant business working as a pot-scrubber and busboy in New York. In July 1858, at the age of twenty-four, Frederick Henry Harvey became a United States citizen in St. Louis, Missouri. Later, he owned a café in St. Louis that catered to wealthy businessmen who expected fast service and good food served in tasteful surroundings. However, the effects of the Civil War and a dishonest partner brought an end to Harvey's first restaurant venture. He then found employment with the railroad as a freight agent, solicitor and mail clerk, traveling many miles by rail. This experience provided firsthand knowledge of how difficult it was to get decent food while traveling by train. This knowledge would serve him and future railroad passengers very well.

Harvey was aware of the plans for expansion of the Atchison, Topeka & Santa Fe (ATSF) railroad and understood the need to develop a robust passenger business to finance the growth. With his knowledge of the restaurant business, he believed he could help accomplish this. When Harvey met with Santa Fe officials in 1876, the entrepreneur was confident he could personally change the miserable reputation of railway dining and increase passenger service. On a handshake with the president of the Santa Fe, an agreement was reached, and the first restaurant chain in the United States was launched.

Left: Fred Harvey, founder of Harvey House restaurants, newsstands and hotels. Harvey is credited for bringing a high standard of hospitality to towns along the Santa Fe Railroad from Kansas to California. *Courtesy of kansasmemory.org, Kansas State Historical Society.*

Below: Early photo of the Fred Harvey family home in Leavenworth, Kansas. Efforts are underway to preserve the historic home. *Courtesy of Tom Taylor.*

As Harvey's chain of trackside restaurants grew, when a location was deemed appropriate for a Harvey establishment, the Santa Fe would design and build space in or adjacent to the new depot building for the kitchen, food storage, a lunch counter and usually a dining room as well as living quarters for Harvey employees. This space, specially built for Harvey's business venture, would become known as a Harvey House. Harvey was also afforded the use of Santa Fe trains to deliver laundry, food products and employees along the line at no charge.

Originally, Harvey Houses were established along the railroad at intervals of approximately one hundred miles, providing dining opportunities for passengers when the train stopped to refuel the steam engine. Other sites were determined by the locations of Santa Fe division points, where large numbers of railroad employees needed a place to eat.

It is often stated that Fred Harvey civilized the West; however, I agree with Philip F. Anschutz's assessment of Harvey in his book, *Out Where the West Begins*. Anschutz included Harvey in this volume of "profiles, visions and strategies of early Western business leaders" along with other notable businessmen such as Henry Ford, J.P. Morgan and Texas cattleman Charles Goodnight. The author writes that "Harvey's dining and tourism dynasty introduced the West to new forms of civilization, powerfully influencing our popular imagination to this very day."

Referring to the famous Harvey Girls, Anschutz wrote that historians "have noted how Harvey's hiring practices represented an important opportunity for single young women. Not since the beginning of the Massachusetts textile industry in the 1820s had American girls seen such a chance to break away from their parents' control and make a living on their own."

The Fred Harvey company valued consistent food quality as much as quality of service. Well-paid European chefs were hired and installed in every Harvey kitchen. Gradually, as lesser kitchen staff could be trained to prepare meals that met the Harvey standard, the chefs were sent to the larger Harvey hotel restaurants. Only the best, freshly prepared food was offered at a Harvey House, and travelers soon realized they could trust the Harvey name all along the Santa Fe line.

In the early years, the Harvey organization centralized its menu selections. Menus were planned in four-day increments, printed in the Kansas City, Missouri office and distributed along the line in such a way that train passengers traveling a long distance were presented with a variety of entree selections. In some locations, the menu was hand-lettered on site but still followed the menu planned by the home office. In later years,

Harvey Girl Josephine Long Brewer worked in California and Arizona from 1914 to 1916. *Courtesy of Susan Meinhardt.*

possibly to cater more to tourists, some local managers were allowed to select menu items.

Once Harvey Houses were established across the Southwest, a special Fred Harvey refrigerated boxcar was shuttled twice a week between Los Angeles and Kansas City to supply Harvey Houses with California fruits and vegetables on the eastbound run and the best Kansas City meats on the return trip.

William Allen White, Pulitzer Prize–winning publisher of the *Emporia Gazette*, believed that Fred Harvey's food raised the standard for home-cooked food in America: "Men who have eaten at Fred Harvey's eating houses have come home and insisted on having their meats broiled, not fried; their roasts roasted, not boiled; their potatoes decently cooked and their biscuits light."

Harvey House restaurant managers were required to send tabulated reports to the Harvey headquarters in Kansas City, Missouri, at the end of each day. The purpose of these reports was not to assess possible ways of reducing expenses but to ensure that the Harvey standard was maintained. *Santa Fe* magazine explained that the reports made certain "the slices of ham in the Harvey sandwiches are as thick as ever and the same thickness everywhere and that the coffee is as strong as it should be." (This debunks an oft-told Fred Harvey quote, "Cut the ham thinner," and supports those who reported his final advice as being "Don't cut the ham too thin.") In Harvey Houses, whole pies were cut into four servings instead of the usual six or eight offered in other restaurants. The daily reports reflected the inventory of food used in relation to the number of customers served, indicating that portions were up to Harvey standards. Even when food costs such as meat or dairy prices increased for the Harvey company, menu prices stayed the same. It is believed that many Harvey Houses operated in the red for years. Fred Harvey's business philosophy was simple—he believed that profits would come in the long run if excellent service were provided and maintained.

The Harvey managers were often chosen from existing newsstand managers or cashiers and transferred within the structure. The Harvey system was set up much like that of the Santa Fe, with managers reporting to a superintendent in charge of a certain territory. In each territory, traveling inspectors and auditors were constantly inspecting the hotels and restaurants to ensure they maintained the Harvey standard of service. The superintendent reported to the Harvey office in Kansas City. In the early days, Fred Harvey might have been one of the traveling inspectors, and Harvey House staff had various codes used by train conductors to telegraph a warning that "the boss" was on the next arriving train.

An eloquent fan of the Santa Fe and Fred Harvey, Elbert Hubbard wrote the following review of the two companies in 1909: "The railroad company builds for the future. These men, with prophetic vision, know that the traffic will eventually warrant the expenditure, even if it does not now. They set their stakes and the world comes to them. Thus does the Octopus [the railroad] do for civilization what your detached and individual citizens can never do for themselves." And using Hubbard's analogy, indeed, the successful "octopus" that was the Fred Harvey company made its way across northern Arizona all the way to the West Coast.

Just before the turn of the twentieth century, Fred Harvey's restaurant and hotel business was prospering, and as the only railroad line offering this level of service to its passengers, the ATSF was experiencing an increase in profits, too. The railroad executives were so pleased with their Harvey partnership that, in 1889, they granted Fred Harvey a "sweetheart contract" giving him the monopoly of all dining sites on the ATSF line.

Perhaps the most important provision granted Harvey in this contract was the exclusive right of food procurement west of the Missouri River. Harvey was granted this exclusive right, with some minor reservations, to manage and operate the "eating houses, lunch stands, and hotel facilities which the company then owned, leased, or was to lease at any time in the future upon any of its railroads west of the Missouri River, including all lines then leased or operated in the name of the Atchison, Topeka and Santa Fe. Coal, ice, and water were to be provided by the railroad; employees and supplies were to be hauled free. Profits, arising from the operations were to go to Fred Harvey in full for all services rendered by him in such business."

That same year, a chain of events began that threatened the partnership between Fred Harvey and the ATSF. Although the partnership between Harvey and the railroad is generally portrayed as a congenial collaboration, after Allen Manvel became president of the ATSF in September 1889, he initiated plans for dining car service west of Kansas City. Fred Harvey was not part of this plan.

Two years later, Fred Harvey filed suit in Chicago attempting to restrain the Atchison, Topeka & Santa Fe Railway from running or operating dining cars along the line west of the Missouri River. The legal action stated that the ATSF had violated the contract with Harvey to supply passengers with meals in trackside restaurants by operating dining cars from Chicago to Denver. Harvey obtained an injunction enjoining the railroad company from interfering with his business and refusing to stop at his eating establishments. He claimed that his restaurants had cost him over $100,000. An interesting note here: Judge W.C. Hook, of Cook County, who granted the restraining order, was a close personal friend of Harvey and served as an honorary pallbearer at Harvey's funeral ten years later.

The suit dragged on for several years, during which Manvel backed off from his ATSF dining car business plan. Soon after this breach in the "sweetheart deal" between Harvey and the railway company, the ATSF went into receivership; however, even during this period, Fred Harvey prospered. After the reorganization of the railroad company, then–ATSF president Edward P. Ripley reached a contract agreement with Harvey that was finalized in 1899. Soon, Santa Fe advertising began to tout its dining car service as being "under management of Mr. Fred Harvey."

There were other signs that Fred Harvey and the ATSF were "playing nice" again. To ensure that no passengers missed the train, it became common practice in the early 1900s for the train conductors to call departing trains in the depot waiting rooms—men's and ladies'—as well as in the Harvey House. This courtesy eliminated any anxiety a diner might have about missing his train.

The excellence of service provided by the ATSF was attributed to the single ownership and management of the line. This same principle applied to the restaurant and dining car service under the management of Fred Harvey. The Harvey system offered superior quality throughout—the best equipment, well-trained employees and an emphasis on customer service.

In response to a 1902 train excursion embarked upon by the Texas Federation of Women's Clubs, the organization's president, Mrs. Percy V. Pennypacker, purchased ads in Arizona newspapers: "We wish to express our appreciation of the excellent service of the SANTA FE road; of the management; of the special train; of the courtesy of every official from superintendent to porter; of the perfection of the Harvey Eating Houses. May the Santa Fe live long and prosper."

Special "heavy-roast" Fred Harvey coffee was a favorite of Harvey House customers in every location. Harvey Girls were required to prepare fresh coffee every two hours. The company's annual report for 1907 showed that 300,000 pounds of coffee were brewed that year. Fred Harvey coffee was also available to take home. The company marketing encouraged customers to do this by distributing printed instructions for brewing the best coffee: "The secrets of good coffee are that it be 1) made strong enough, 2) served hot enough, 3) brewed correctly, 4) always freshly made and 5) made from good coffee." Following these points, specific

Following Fred Harvey's specifications, Harvey Girls brewed fresh coffee every two hours.
Courtesy of Special Collections, University of Arizona Libraries, Fred Harvey collection (AZ 326).

instructions were given on how to successfully make Fred Harvey coffee at home whether you prepared drip coffee, percolator coffee or used a glass coffee maker or an automatic coffee maker.

Fred Harvey was often described as high-strung and demanding. His strict rules for his employees, especially Harvey Girls, are well known. This set of rules posted in Harvey employee living quarters is dated 1887:

> *Employees are requested not to scratch matches, drive nails or tacks, or any other way mar the walls of their rooms.*
>
> *No rubbish of any kind must be thrown in the toilets.*
>
> *Bath tubs* [sic] *must be thoroughly cleaned by employes* [sic] *after using.*
>
> *Loud talking and laughing in rooms and halls should be avoided.*
>
> *Employes* [sic] *must be in their rooms by 11:00 o'clock p.m. unless given special permission by manager to remain out longer.*
>
> *Rooms must be kept in tidy condition and wearing apparel must be kept in its proper place.*

Expectorating on floors is positively forbidden.
The purpose of the above rules is to bring about a tidy and homelike
condition in your rooms and we request your co-operation [sic] *so that the*
desired results will be brought about.
Fred Harvey

Harvey had high expectations for his customers as well as his employees. For many years, every Harvey House had a "coat rule" requiring male patrons to wear a coat if they were eating in the dining room. The requirement was challenged in 1921 by the Corporate Commission of the State of Oklahoma. The commission claimed the Harvey rule showed discrimination among patrons; however, the appellate court ordered this decision overturned, and the coat rule stood. Most Harvey House managers had a few dark coats in various sizes set aside to accommodate a gentleman diner who arrived without a coat. A man having to wear a coat while eating a meal, even in warm weather, must have seemed silly to some in remote rural towns, and enforcing the coat rule was surely a challenge when cowboys showed up carrying guns.

The Fred Harvey "coat rule" was suspended in the dining room of the El Garces in Needles, California, due to the extreme heat, and there were instances when creative, hungry men found a way around the rule. The *Arizona Republic* newspaper shared such a situation that occurred in Winslow, Arizona, in the early twentieth century. A large number of cowboys rode into town having just finished a long cattle drive. The men had been eating beans and jerky for two weeks and had their sights set on a delicious meal at the Harvey House served by fetching Harvey Girls. Alas, when they arrived, they were met by the manager, who informed them that coats were required in the dining room. The tired and dusty cowboys were not going to settle for the light meal offered at the lunch counter, so they went out to their horses, and each cowboy put on his yellow, boot-length rain slicker. Once again, they entered the lobby of the Harvey House and declared, "Now, sir, we are wearing coats!" The manager chuckled and allowed the men to enter, offering to serve them "anything you want, compliments of Harvey House."

By the early 1960s, the Fred Harvey company and its employee rules had, of course, changed considerably, as had travel and the experience of eating in a restaurant. Employees no longer lived under Harvey's roof. An employee manual distributed in the early 1960s contained standard information regarding vacations, payday, overtime pay and safety. However, the message in the first paragraphs of the manual is reminiscent of the early Harvey days, when, many years after Mr. Harvey's death, employees still declared, "I work for Fred Harvey":

> *Each and every employee and the job he or she does is vital to the continued success of Fred Harvey and we are glad to have you with us. We want you to feel at home, to be happy in your work and to be glad that you have joined our family.*
>
> *Fred Harvey is known internationally for good food, for fine and friendly service and for the charm of our restaurants, shops and hotels. These basic principles were behind the founding of the first Harvey House in the railroad depot at Topeka, Kan., in 1876 and they are just as important now as they were in the beginning.*
>
> *Wherever one finds Fred Harvey…whether at Chicago's luxurious Kungsholm, at wonderful old El Tovar at the Grand Canyon, at the Pavilion in Los Angeles' Music Center or at the Oasis restaurants on the Illinois tollway…one finds the same spirit of hospitality and gracious service.*
>
> *Let's take just a minute or two to think about COURTESY. After all, courtesy or thoughtfulness and concern for others is the key to a successful relationship with our guests and with our co-workers* [sic].

The front cover of this employee manual has an illustration of a family dressed in typical 1960s fashion exiting a Harvey House restaurant. The exterior of the restaurant looks very much like an orange-roofed Howard Johnson restaurant, a successful restaurant/hotel chain during the 1960s and 1970s. However, a section of the employee manual with "basic information for those of you who have joined the ranks of the world's most famous group of waitresses" is illustrated with a drawing of a Harvey Girl in a traditional, ankle-length black-and-white uniform. Almost a century after its inception, the Fred Harvey company was still clinging to the positive public reputation of the Harvey Girl:

> *The success of the first Fred Harvey restaurant and of every other Fred Harvey restaurant since that time has been largely dependent upon the fine job done by these young ladies…or Harvey Girls as they have always been known.*
>
> *You are the person who represents Fred Harvey to our guests. If they are pleased with you and with your service they are pleased with Fred Harvey. If they are unhappy with you there is very little the company can do about it.*

It is no exaggeration to say that not only your own job but the success of the HARVEY HOUSE itself depends upon you.
Our guests will be interested in:
Your appearance
Your attitude
Your service
And if you do the sort of job that these guests have come to expect from a HARVEY GIRL, you will be rewarded in a number of ways.

Once the historical pride of the Harvey Girl had been established, a photograph of the 1960s Harvey waitress uniform with the hem coming just below the knee accompanied company rules about personal appearance:

Take pride in your appearance. Look professional in your grooming.
Bathe daily before coming to work and follow your bath with the application of an effective deodorant.
Wear fresh, clean lingerie.
Keep your hands and nails clean.
Be sure of a clean, sweet breath through proper daily care of your teeth and the use of a mouth wash or gargle.
Have clean hair, simply dressed and covered with a hair net.
Use make-up lightly, emphasizing a natural look.
Always take one last critical look in the mirror. Remember that a smile on your face is also a part of the Harvey Girl uniform.

Numerous former Harvey staff members came out of retirement to help feed American soldiers and foreign prisoners of war transported by train across the United States during World War II. This was a difficult experience for the former Harvey employees. The work was exhausting, and the ideals set forth by Fred Harvey many years before were sacrificed to meet the demands of serving and preparing hundreds of meals each day. Linen tablecloths were abandoned; however, linen napkins were still used. Meals were no longer cooked to order; instead, food was prepared in large quantities and kept warm throughout the day. Many of the menu items offered when Harvey Houses were thriving were unavailable during wartime due to food rationing.

Modifications were made throughout the Harvey system, such as converting the Indian curio room at Fray Marcos hotel in Williams, Arizona, into a sandwich shop to help serve the troops. The improvised fast-food service area employed three Harvey Girls and one Harvey Sandwich Boy and served up to 1,400 sandwiches a day.

During this same time, Fred Harvey was using magazine advertising to put a positive spin on changes that occurred while the company was serving the troop trains. One ad shows a drawing of an older woman with a picture of a Harvey Girl in the background. The headline, "Back in the ranks…" leads into the copy, "and she's always on call to help in a pinch at Fred Harvey's—the same Harvey House where she was a Harvey Girl forty years ago. Except for patriotic women like her, many of our young fighting men would go hungry." The ad further explains that "to do this job and do it well—in spite of help shortages, rationing and our greatly increased civilian patronage—is now our foremost task. If this occasionally means we cannot give you the old-time Fred Harvey service, we know you understand. When our war job is done we promise you only Harvey hospitality at its very best."

In reality, the thousands of troops traveling by train added greatly to the Harvey House customer base at a time when civilian train travel was waning, bringing profits back to some sites that had been closed for several years. The results of a smart, extensive marketing effort—coupled with the enduring Harvey reputation and an increase in patrons—were very positive for the company. According to intercompany memos, Fred Harvey served over forty-one million meals and brought in a gross income of over $37 million in 1945, the largest in the company's seventy-year history.

In a variety of ways throughout the history of Fred Harvey and the Santa Fe Railway, the companies relied on the enduring reputation of Harvey Girls for positive marketing material. In the spring of 1950, a decline in business prompted the general traffic manager of the Santa Fe, R.T. Anderson, to announce a plan to revive interest in Harvey hospitality. "Harvey Girls are returning to the Southwest." The idea was to appeal to vacation travelers who might enjoy "a more leisurely type of trip through the Indian country of New Mexico and Arizona." While the announcement most likely stirred quite a bit of interest from train-travel enthusiasts, a return to the golden days of Harvey House dining never happened.

Fred Harvey suffered from cancer for over fifteen years and died at the age of sixty-five in 1901. Company documents show that in that same year, Harvey owned and operated fifteen hotels, forty-seven restaurants, thirty dining cars and a San Francisco Bay ferry.

This eulogy, prepared by Elbert Hubbard, popular writer and publisher, was a sincere tribute to Fred Harvey; however, looking back, we see it as an appropriate description of what the name "Fred Harvey" would mean for many years to come:

> *Fred Harvey? Do you know the name? If not, then your education has been much neglected. Fred Harvey used to run a restaurant. He ran it so well that the Santa Fe railroad folks got him to establish a line of restaurants along the road from Chicago to California, and also down into Texas. Some say that the Santa Fe made Fred Harvey, but the fact is, Fred Harvey had a little something to do with making the Santa Fe Railroad.*
>
> *Fred Harvey set a standard of excellence! It is a terrible thing to acquire a Fred Harvey reputation. Where the name, Fred Harvey, appears, the traveling public expects much. It may be on the desert of Arizona, a hundred miles from water, but if it is a Fred Harvey place, you get filtered spring water, ice, fresh fruit and every other good thing that you can find at the same season in the best places in New York or Chicago. How the miracle occurs you do not know—it is a Fred Harvey concern—that is enough!*
>
> *And so this man, Fred Harvey, has educated thousands of young men and women, and showed them how to meet people, how to serve them without boring them, how to speed them on their way in gladness.*
>
> *Fred Harvey is dead, but his spirit still lives. The standard of excellence he set can never go back. He has been a civilizer and benefactor. He has added to the physical, mental, and spiritual welfare of millions. No sermon can equal a Fred Harvey example—no poet can better a Fred Harvey precept. Fred Harvey simply kept faith with the public. He gave pretty nearly a perfect service. I did not know Fred Harvey, but I know this: he must have been an honest man, a good man—for the kind of a business a man builds up is a reflection of himself—spun out of his heart. Man, like Deity, creates in his own image. I take off my hat to Fred Harvey, who served the patrons of the Santa Fe so faithfully and well, that dying, he yet lives, his name a symbol of all that is honest, excellent, hygienic, beautiful and useful.*

After Fred Harvey's death, his sons Ford and Byron continued to operate the substantial family business and were very successful in expanding the business into Arizona and, in particular, the Grand Canyon. The decision was made for the company name to simply be "Fred Harvey," maintaining the illusion that the founder was still alive. For years after Fred Harvey's death, employees continued to say they worked for Fred Harvey; in correspondence and printed marketing pieces, the company was referred to as "Fred Harvey."

Ford Harvey, Fred's oldest son, left Racine College in Wisconsin after three years because of his father's failing health and to begin working in the Harvey company's Kansas City, Missouri offices. Ford had a variety of responsibilities and learned his father's business well. There was some speculation that Ford, who was appointed president of the company after his father's death, may have chosen the company name because of a lack of self-confidence. However, with experience from working beside his father for many years and a decisive manner of conducting business, I'm inclined to believe Ford realized this would be a smart marketing tactic. And it was!

Almost fifteen years after his father's death, Ford was recognized for his "executive qualifications and business ability" by the Missouri newspaper the *Independent*:

> *Ford P. Harvey leaves an eighteen carat hall mark* [sic] *on his record as a business man. Since his elevation to the head of the great Harvey system its expansion and growth has been of the most stable and progressive character. The achievements of his father have been doubly complimented by respectful acknowledgement, and by a continued uplifting of standards. In fact, the regime of the Harvey system, under the son's presidency has been a question of ideals. Ford Harvey is peculiarly lacking in personal ambition. Even his identity is obscure to the general public to whom only the name Fred Harvey is familiar. And he has lost sight of ambition for the great big successful business which he operates in his determination to make and keep it at the highest possible standard.*

Fred Harvey's sons established separate offices—Ford in Kansas City and Byron in Chicago. During this time, Ford was responsible for hotels, restaurants, newsstands and shops, and Byron managed the railroad dining cars.

Until the end of the nineteenth century, Harvey House buildings were of inexpensive frame construction, built for efficiency. In the early 1900s, Ford Harvey and Santa Fe president Edward P. Ripley began to consider building new railroad depots and Harvey establishments reminiscent of the Spanish Colonial–Indian pueblo style of architecture. The men agreed on a plan that called for construction of a system-wide series of approximately twenty trackside hotels, some of which would be regional in design. The railroad architects would continue to participate in the design of the new buildings; however, others, such as Louis Curtiss of Kansas City, were also commissioned to design the buildings and supervise construction.

In an interview shortly before his death in 1928, Ford explained the difficulties of operating Harvey Houses:

> *With us it is the task of seeing to it that every long-distance passenger upon the railroads that we serve has proper food accommodations for the entire duration of his journey. We have to meet the tastes and whims of all sorts and conditions of men—those to whom a trip across the continent is ordinary routine, and those who are on a train for the first time. I have found the most-traveled man makes the least fuss about what we serve him. It is the untraveled person who is apt to be the most exacting. Yet he or she is entitled none the less to the very best service that we can possibly render.*
>
> *A man may have only thirty cents to pay for a meal, but we must treat him with the same deference and courtesy as if he were paying ten times that amount. He may not tip the waitress in the lunchroom. That often happens. It is our business, however, to keep that employe [sic] just as well satisfied as if she had received a generous tip, so that the next time that man comes over the road—our people have an uncanny way of remembering and of recognizing them—they will render him just as good service as if he had established a reputation along the line as a generous giver.*
>
> *We create the very best working conditions—wages, hours, surroundings—that we can possibly devise for our people, by working with them all the time, never letting them remain in the dark as to our plans or as to our methods, and then by letting them feel that the hotel or restaurant of which they may be in charge is, for the time being at least, theirs, not ours.*

Following Ford's death, Byron Harvey became president of the Fred Harvey company and continued in that capacity until his death in 1954.

There are many letters in Fred Harvey company archives written by satisfied customers over the years. Often, Ford or Byron Harvey would circulate copies of the letters to Harvey managers, urging them to carry on the company standards. According to an article in the *Santa Fe Employes'* [sic] magazine in 1910, the following letter, written by H.R. Pattengill of Michigan, was quoted in the editorial columns of a number of newspapers in the southwest:

> *Nearly forty days of travel and experience along the Santa Fe, and corresponding familiarity with the Harvey eating-house system, leads us to pay this tribute to its force of dining-room girls. In all this time, in a score of different hotels, and of the hundreds of waiters, the editor did not see any*

unladylike or flippant action. The young ladies were, without exception, neat and becomingly attired, courteous and expert in their work, dignified yet cheery, bright eyed, clear faced and intelligent. It is also worthy of note that they received from the thousands of guests whom they served the courtesy which their bearing demanded. Some of the traveling show troupe women, with their bepowdered, enameled, ready-made complexions, peroxide puffs, wienerwurst curls, loud talk and louder behavior, might well get some wholesome lessons in womanliness from the Harvey House waitresses.

Ahead of its time, the Fred Harvey company was establishing its brand over a century before "branding" became a buzzword. Fred Harvey fruit preserves were served at breakfast. For a time, Coca-Cola bottles produced in Newton, Kansas, had the imprint "Fred Harvey Newton" on the bottom. Harvey Houses are credited with originating the "blue-plate special," a daily, low-priced, complete meal that was served on a blue-patterned china plate. An 1892 Harvey menu mentions this dining option some thirty years before it became a common restaurant term. In the United States, until the early 1960s, when the country's eating habits began to change, ordering the blue-plate or daily special in a café or diner meant you got a meal predetermined by the restaurant and usually consisting of meat, vegetables and bread served on one plate for a reduced price.

The Fred Harvey logo, composed simply of Harvey's name, was attached to high-quality products such as coffee, whiskey and cigars as well as on menus and signage. Some have credited Mary Colter for transforming Harvey's actual signature into the company logo. An architect who had a long career with Fred Harvey, Colter is recognized as the designer of many Harvey Houses, including El Tovar, Bright Angel Lodge and Phantom Ranch headquarters providing tourist accommodations at the Grand Canyon.

Whenever possible, the Fred Harvey company encouraged publicity about its food and hotel service with the use of well-placed newspaper and magazine articles. An oft-used phrase was that Fred Harvey "set the desert abloom with beefsteaks." A 1940s article printed in the *American Mercury* magazine and reprinted in *Reader's Digest* cleverly described Fred Harvey as "turning a shoestring potato into a 2,500-mile string of railroad eating places." The article also said that Harvey "unconsciously launched a 'matrimonial bureau' which played a major role in civilizing the Southwest." All along the route of the Santa Fe, "you can talk with fine young college men and girls who are proud that Mother once worked for Fred Harvey and met Dad over the pie counter."

The imposing Harvey hotel, El Tovar, overlooks the Grand Canyon train depot in this postcard photograph. *Courtesy of Michael McMillan.*

The decline in Harvey Houses beginning in the 1930s has been attributed to several factors. One is the increase in the number of dining cars, which allowed passengers to enjoy delicious, well-prepared meals in comfortable surroundings without leaving the train. Even in the late 1800s, Fred Harvey dining car service was competing with his trackside restaurants. In the fall of 1897, the ATSF announced that the fast California Limited train would resume its service. The passenger train would make the run through Kansas across the country to Los Angeles in fifty-four hours. Described as a "hotel on wheels," it provided passengers with dinner in Kansas, breakfast in Colorado, lunch in New Mexico, dinner the second day in Arizona and breakfast and lunch in California without leaving the train. A first-class, one-way ticket cost thirty dollars (meals not included).

The Fred Harvey restaurant system eventually had to move to where most passengers went—airports and resorts. In 1968, the company supervised food service on the dining cars of the Santa Fe Railway in an operation that extended over thirteen thousand miles of railroad track. Many Harvey locations had closed, but hubs such as Chicago's Union Station remained important because of a concentration of commuter traffic. A company report stated that approximately a dozen Harvey restaurants and gift shops were still operating at that time.

The Fred Harvey company became a subsidiary of Amfac, Inc., in 1968. To some extent, the Harvey influence remained intact with Fred's grandsons Daggett and Stewart Harvey serving on the Amfac board of directors for a time. Of course, many things changed, and this transaction was not well received by former Harvey employees who had been loyal to Fred Harvey. Opal Sells Hill, a Harvey Girl veteran of forty-five years, recalled, "When Amfac took over Harvey, everyone was told, 'Throw out them Harvey Girl uniforms.' And they did. What a shame!"

After a merger in the early 1990s, all that remained of the Fred Harvey company became part of Xanterra, the largest parks concession management company in the United States. On its website, www.xanterra. com, the company refers to the Fred Harvey proven expertise and Xanterra's commitment to those principles in today's hospitality business.

2

THOSE WINSOME HARVEY GIRLS

As Fred Harvey's vision for first-class eating establishments along the Santa Fe Railroad became a reality, there were challenges, with the most predominate being the difficulty of finding employees who would maintain the Harvey standards.

In small railroad towns, the population didn't provide many folks to consider for Harvey employment. The prevailing story of how the idea of Harvey Girls unfolded takes place in Raton, New Mexico. In 1882, when a Harvey House was established in this remote northern New Mexico town, an all-male staff served the patrons consisting mostly of miners, cowboys and railroad men. Following an after-hours fight involving the staff, no one was able to work the next morning. When word of the situation reached Fred Harvey, he took the train to Raton to remedy the situation. An enraged Harvey fired everyone and hired a new manager, Tom Gable. Gable proposed replacing the disorderly men with attractive young women, correctly reasoning that the women would be more reliable and cause less trouble. He believed the change in staff would also be well received by train passengers and the community. Harvey agreed. Using popular women's magazines and newspapers, he placed ads such as this to entice qualified young women to apply to work for Fred Harvey: "Wanted—Young women, 18–30 years of age, of good character, attractive, and intelligent, as waitresses in Harvey Eating Houses on the Santa Fe Railroad in the West. Good wages, with room and meals furnished. Experience not necessary. Write Fred Harvey, Union Depot, Kansas City, Missouri." Kansas Harvey House history, however,

Jeannie Williams was a Harvey Girl at the Havasu in Seligman, Arizona, in the early 1920s. *Courtesy of Old Trails Museum and Winslow Historical Society.*

lists women, including a Harvey relative, as waitresses as early as 1880, two years before the Raton incident.

Thousands of ambitious young women who passed the rigorous personal interview at the Kansas City, Missouri—or, later, Chicago, Illinois—Harvey offices were given a train pass to their new jobs and often left immediately. Some were sent home and, weeks later, received a letter on Fred Harvey stationery requesting that they report to work.

The company only accepted women who presented themselves well—neatly dressed and groomed—and who spoke clearly and showed good manners. Harvey wasn't looking for experienced waitresses, as the company wanted to train their new hires in the strict "Harvey way." In the early years, all Harvey Girls were single and were required to sign a contract stipulating they would not marry during the first six months of employment. Between 1883 and the late 1950s, company records state that approximately 100,000 Harvey Girls proudly wore the now-famous black-and-white uniforms.

Alice Steele began her career with the Fred Harvey company in 1910, at age twenty-one, as a file clerk and later moved into the employment department as an assistant, eventually taking sole charge of hiring in the Kansas City office. In a newspaper interview, Steele described her work as "interesting to me because I am in sympathy with the position. I have one great ambition, and that is to uphold the name of Fred Harvey, and with this always in mind I cannot engage employees who are not a credit to the firm. One of the greatest pleasures of my work is making the new employees feel that someone is taking an interest in them." She further explained her commitment to new employees: "I never let them think for a moment that after hiring them and giving them their transportation to their place of employment I dismiss them from my mind. I write to them, and encourage them to write to me, and, as far as I consistently can do it, I arrange to give the girls the station they desire." Steele expressed an understanding that "a girl who is lonely in Chicago and not at her best may give ideal service in a little town where she soon makes friends with everybody."

An article that appeared in the *Hartford Courant* in 1923 correctly gave Alice Steele credit for the success of Harvey Girls throughout the Harvey system. "It has been said in a popular novel that the girls who serve in the string of Fred Harvey eating houses trailing from Chicago across the Great Desert to the Pacific coast, are the smartest girls in the world, which gives added interest to the woman—a girl herself, who hires them." The story describes the seemingly simple process that changed the lives of so many young women. "Her name is Alice Steele, and before her desk in the Kansas City Union Station there passes for inspection every person seeking a position with the great Fred Harvey system."

During her first ten years as employment manager, Steele is credited with interviewing and hiring not only potential Harvey Girls but also "pantry women, cooks, bakers, porters, cleaners—all the help needed around hotels."

Most likely, Alice Steele's commitment to Fred Harvey principles contributed to her successful employment with the company. She realized that experience as a waitress was not a requirement for a successful Harvey Girl. "Waitresses are recruited from almost every line of business. Sometimes girls realize that life in a stuffy office is not living at all; sometimes they grow tired of the routine of teaching school; sometimes they find they are failures financially in the handcrafts; often students seek employment during the summer to give them both an income and the out of doors they need. As our hours are not long this is possible in a Harvey eating house." Looking back through the eyes of experienced Harvey Girls who expressed the demands of twelve-hour shifts in a Harvey House, perhaps Steele should have stated that hours in a Harvey House were flexible rather than "not long."

It is obvious from interviews with Steele that she had a clear understanding of the motivation of young women she was to consider for employment and appreciated the individual attributes they could bring to the job. "We have many girls who are actuated by the wanderlust." At one time, there were two sisters from Central America on the payroll. "They were well educated, speaking five languages. They had spent four years in foreign countries, and wished to see the West. They had paid their way around the world serving as waitresses, and ranked among the best we had ever had."

Steele kept a card catalog history of every applicant that she hired. The information included the employee's name, hometown, nationality, age, physical qualifications and occupation. Later, Steele would add reports concerning the service given. Habits, good or bad, were noted, as well as if the applicant was discharged and when and why. The employment manager noted that a great many Harvey Girls married. "This is not surprising, for they are uniformly of pleasing personality, and their work is in a section where there is no discouraging the seeking of a husband."

Alice Steele is remembered fondly by some Harvey Girls as being sympathetic and understanding. One Harvey Girl remembered that if she didn't get back to Kansas City for five years and then would go into Steele's office, Alice would call her by name. "With hundreds of girls to deal with, she never forgot one and always was friendly." However, other hopeful Harvey Girls found Steele to be stern and somewhat harsh. In either case, this initial interview looms large in the memory of many Harvey Girls.

Because she was the employment manager, Steele's impression of a young lady determined whether the black-and-white uniform would be in her future in far-flung locations as the Santa Fe expanded passenger service toward California. Many young women made their way to Kansas City for an interview, but Alice often had to resort to actively recruiting Harvey Girls. A 1920 report in the *Abilene Weekly Chronicle* stated that "the Fred Harvey eating house system faces a curtailment because of a shortage of 'Harvey House' girls, according to Alice Steele of Kansas City, who is trying to recruit an army of girl helpers. Marriage was the culprit. Even though Harvey Girls signed an agreement to work at least six months before leaving the job, following the end of World War I, Steele reported that of two thousand women employed through her office in 1919, twelve hundred had quit to become brides." Alice even traveled to other states during this time, often visiting small towns to enlist women for all departments of the Harvey system. Later, as the West became more populated and trusted Harvey managers were in place, more local women were hired.

The young women who answered Fred Harvey's classified ads did so for many different reasons. Some were simply looking for a way to leave the family farm and explore the possibilities of a different kind of life. Others realized the money they could make as a Harvey Girl would pay for the education required for a career in teaching or nursing. Mabel Hawkinson described the benefits of her Harvey Girl career in a letter. "I started in Kansas City and after working a short time in Dodge City, Kansas moved on up the line to Gallup, New Mexico and then to the Grand Canyon. I made good money, had lots of fun along with a lot of hard work. I loved it. I later married a farmer and stockman. Even now that I've been retired a long time I'm not pinched for money."

Some applicants were simply looking for adventure. Surely, all the Harvey Girl hopefuls were keenly aware that working in a remote place where few women lived would provide opportunities for meeting a prospective husband. If, somehow, this possibility escaped a young woman, newspaper and magazine articles often emphasized this benefit with phrases such as: "Sensible girls got their men by going where the men were."

Harvey Girls personalized the Fred Harvey standards and brought their eastern and midwestern sensibilities to a job that previously had not been held in high esteem. Harvey's strict rules about dressing modestly, wearing little or no makeup and conducting oneself in a respectable manner served the purpose of reassuring the young ladies they would be in good company working and living with likeminded women. Their reputations would be protected even far from home, where they would be judged without benefit of a family's good reputation. Often, the Harvey House manager would designate a parlor or other space for the exclusive use of Harvey employees. This provided an acceptable place where Harvey Girls and their guests could meet socially.

At the time early Harvey Girls were hired, workingwomen were often scorned unless they were teachers or nurses. Waitressing, in particular, was considered one of the lowest professions a woman could choose and was generally not considered a proper profession for a white, middle-class

Three unidentified Harvey Girls in traditional 1918 uniforms at the Winslow, Arizona Harvey House. *Courtesy of Old Trails Museum and Winslow Historical Society.*

young woman. In the unsettled West, many waitresses were also prostitutes, and even when this was not true, the perception prevailed. Usually, tough, coarse women were the only ones who could make it alone in remote, rural areas. The sheltered living circumstances provided for Harvey Girls made it possible for more refined women to survive in uncivilized and/or developing railroad towns.

Fred Harvey's rules were a dominant part of any Harvey Girl's experience, but they served many good purposes. In addition to providing a protective atmosphere for the women, the rules standardized service in Harvey Houses and helped sell the Harvey ideal all along the Santa Fe. Just as Fred Harvey changed the standards for food and service for train passengers, he changed the standards for the job of a waitress. Harvey Girls were expected to conduct themselves in a ladylike manner at all times. This conduct changed the public perception of working, single women—especially waitresses.

Serving procedures were standardized throughout the Harvey system, and Harvey Girls usually had to train for a month before they were given their own tables or lunch counter seats to serve. In the beginning, newcomers usually squeezed orange juice or cut the butter into squares, but they would soon be following another Harvey Girl and learning the proper way to interact with guests. Generally, the young women did not receive pay during this training time. If a girl couldn't meet the expected standards or decided that a Harvey Girl career wasn't what she wanted, she was given a train pass to go home.

An efficient, somewhat mysterious "cup code" helped streamline the service to harried train passengers. After diners were seated, a waitress would ask whether they preferred coffee, hot tea, iced tea or milk. She would then arrange the cup at the place setting before each patron and move to the next table. Soon, the "drink girl" would arrive at the table and "magically" pour the patron's preferred drink without asking. If the waitress left the cup right side up in its saucer, that meant coffee; upside down meant hot tea; upside down but tilted against the saucer meant iced tea; and upside down and away from the saucer meant milk.

Getting dressed for work may have been the hardest part of the Harvey Girl job, as the uniform standards were exact and inspections frequent. The now familiar black-and-white uniforms were sent to one of the Harvey laundries located in the Grand Canyon; Needles, California; Newton, Kansas; or Temple, Texas. These important, practical links in the Fred Harvey organization handled laundry for the entire Harvey system of restaurants and hotels. At its peak, operating Harvey laundries averaged over one million pieces of laundry each month and, at times, had to utilize other commercial laundries to handle overflow of Harvey Girl uniforms and table linens. One Harvey Girl informed me, "The uniforms would come back clean and starched. All we had to do was iron them. I was living in the lap of luxury!"

For many years, a hairnet and a corset were required, and stiff white collars were attached to the uniform blouse with straight pins made invisible with white pin heads. Surprise inspections were not unusual—the skirt length measured, fingernails checked and, in the early years, verification that a corset was in place. As Fred Harvey's business practices have been scrutinized, some have speculated that the use of pin fasteners on the Harvey Girl uniform rather than buttons promoted the ideal of—to use a more current phrase—teamwork. Even this small detail established the need to work together to accomplish job responsibilities and, along with dormitory-style living accommodations, fostered an attitude of camaraderie among the young women.

Some historians interpret the crisp black-and-white Harvey Girl uniforms as a way of ensuring a standard of decorum and service. Others believe Harvey chose the style to imitate a nun's habit, thus subtly protecting the reputation of the young waitresses. Perhaps the uniforms were meant to remind patrons of a nurse's uniform, which would help establish a perception of professionalism and service. It is possible that by dressing the young women alike, distractions were eliminated, and restaurant guests were more likely to be impressed by the exacting service and delicious food.

Let's not assume that all young women who became Harvey Girls were compliant young women who unquestionably followed the Fred Harvey rules. For the most part, following the Harvey "rules of employment" was considered a compromise for the opportunities—both financial and social—that were available. We know there were many occasions when the overnight kitchen staff would leave the back door unlocked so errant Harvey Girls could

Harvey Girl Matilda "Tillie" Raugh in the lunchroom of the Havasu in Seligman, Arizona. *Courtesy of Don Gray.*

come in past curfew. In 1910, the waitresses at the Harvey House in Winslow, Arizona, objected to an order issued by their manager. The style of the time was to add volume and fullness to hairstyles by pinning a small ball of hair (called a "rat"), contained in a sheer hairnet, under one's natural hair. Considered too glamorous for efficient waitresses, the manager ordered an end to the use of the "rat" and all other hair accessories while on the job except for the large hair bows considered part of the uniform. Resenting the order, the Harvey Girls quit work just as two trains arrived, leaving no one to serve the hungry passengers eager for a meal. Possibly the first and only labor dispute over hair accessories was quickly settled when the manager gingerly walked back on his edict.

Marjorie Whitney's father was a boilermaker for the Santa Fe and was very familiar with the fine reputation held by Harvey Girls. There was no hesitation when his daughter wanted to go to Williams, Arizona, to work as a Harvey Girl at the elegant Fray Marcos Harvey hotel. "I started in Williams in 1940 and wore a totally white uniform with a black bow tie," Marjorie said. "We always had to have a spare one ready, because we had to change even if we only had a little spill on our uniform." Harvey Girl living quarters were on the second floor above the kitchen. "It was nice in the winter because the floor was always warm, but it got very uncomfortable in the summer. There were strict rules, and the door between our living area and the hotel was always locked at 10 p.m." When Marjorie and her roommate (also named Marjorie) worked the late shift that ended at midnight, they would often sneak out to go dancing at the Saltana dance hall. "One of the night chefs would let us back in through the door leading from the kitchen."

Harvey Girls earned a reputation of having civilized the rural towns where they worked through their contributions to church and community activities. Often, a new Harvey Girl would come from poor rural circumstances, yet she would introduce a love for reading or artistic talent to her adopted home. Many farm girls who became part of the Harvey family were thrust into a world where, perhaps for the first time, they were encouraged to be feminine and take pride in their appearance. The transition was easier to accomplish in the clean surroundings of the Harvey Girl living arrangement with plenty of hot water, some privacy and a dresser with a mirror.

For every personal story in this book, there are hundreds more that would help us remember the difficult decisions, adventurous spirit and desire to perform a job with pride that brought young women to Arizona and brought Arizona women to Harvey Houses.

Certainly, Fred Harvey had a unique vision for restaurants along the railroad and was an astute businessman, as were his sons and grandsons who continued the business after Fred's death. However, it was the employees, led by Harvey Girls, who made the Fred Harvey company a success.

It is well established that most young women who came west to work for Fred Harvey married a railroad man, rancher or a fellow Harvey employee and had a family. However, the willingness to hop on a train and travel hundreds of miles to work in an unfamiliar, mostly uncivilized location reveals a certain level of daring that sometimes led to unconventional pursuits after a woman's employment as a Harvey Girl.

Effie Jenks, who grew up in South Dakota, worked as a Harvey Girl in Arizona and New Mexico in the 1920s and later committed her life to the preservation of the ghost town of Bland, New Mexico. Her husband, a mining engineer from England, purchased the town in 1938 soon after he and Effie married with the hope of reinvigorating mining in the narrow canyon. Owning a reputation of being eccentric and drinking Jack Daniel's neat from a fruit jar, Effie appointed herself mayor after her husband's death and lived in Bland for thirty years without electricity or running water until her death in 1983. The town of Bland was destroyed in the Las Conchas fire in 2011.

Most likely the most notorious former Harvey Girl worked in Deming, New Mexico. Mildred Fantetti Clark Cusey was born in 1906 in Kentucky and was orphaned at the age of twelve when her parents died during a flu epidemic. When her sister Florence contracted tuberculosis, Mildred moved with her to Deming, where her sister was admitted to the Holy Cross Sanatorium at Camp Cody. Mildred was hired as a Harvey Girl through the recommendation of a friend with whom she attended church.

One version of what happened after Mildred became a Harvey Girl is that she was transferred to Needles, California, and because of the extremely hot climate, she quit and returned to New Mexico—but not to the Harvey House. Instead, Mildred went to work at a brothel in Silver City, New Mexico. In the 1930s, while still in her twenties, Mildred owned three brothels in Silver City; one in Deming; one in Lordsburg; and one in Laramie, Wyoming. Eventually, her "business establishments" stretched from New Mexico to Alaska.

Mildred later became known as Madam Millie and proved to be a very successful businesswoman. In addition to the many brothels, she also owned a ranch, restaurants and various homes. Mildred was very active in the community and local charities and was once described by a Deming resident as "the most sincere and giving person I ever met." Millie's last husband (of twenty years) was James Wendell Cusey, a naval veteran of World War II, and Millie is buried next to him in the Fort Bayard National Cemetery. While not entirely living up to the wholesome image of a Harvey Girl, Madam Millie was a survivor and certainly made her own place in history.

The life story of one particular Winslow, Arizona Harvey Girl has all of the essentials of a very entertaining movie. At the turn of the twentieth century, another "resourceful" Harvey Girl, Olive Dove Van Zoast, left her home in South Dakota at the age of fourteen to escape an abusive father and unhappy family life. She eventually made her way to Winslow, Arizona, where she applied for work, lied about her age and was hired as a Harvey Girl. She also changed her name to Juanita Gale. After living on the road and working odd jobs for months, she was very appreciative of the provided clean living quarters and the steady paycheck. By all accounts, she was an efficient Harvey Girl, apparently obeying the house rules and handling her responsibilities in an acceptable manner. However, there were sure to be some behind-the-back whispers when, once her shift was over, Juanita dressed in boots and men's jeans and spent her free time either at the horse barn or riding a borrowed horse out into the desert.

Harvey Girls with manager W.E. Belding (*center*) at the Harvey House in Winslow, Arizona, circa 1920. Olive Van Zoast, who later became a rancher known as Cecil Creswell, is third from right. *Courtesy of Old Trails Museum and Winslow Historical Society.*

At this point, there are different versions of the events of Juanita's life, and the exact timeline is blurry, but this is the most consistent account of how things unfolded for this petite, attractive young woman.

Following the tradition of so many Harvey Girls, Juanita met and married a local man and quit her job. Shortly after their marriage, Juanita discovered the man was already married, and ultimately, he was charged with bigamy and sent to prison. After explaining her predicament to the La Posada manager, Juanita was rehired and settled back into her relatively comfortable life as a Harvey Girl. Not much time passed before George Creswell, who regularly ate at La Posada, took notice of Juanita. After a suitable time of "courting," the couple married, and when Juanita changed her last name to Creswell, she also changed her first name to Cecil. George was a livestock inspector with the Bureau of Indian Affairs and owned a small ranch just outside of Winslow. This marriage was a happy one, and with George's steady employment, Cecil enjoyed life on their small ranch. However, this former Harvey Girl's life took another hard turn when George suddenly died, leaving her financially destitute.

As a solution to her situation, Cecil married a man with the improbable name of Moon Mullins. Not long after their wedding, Moon took a job as a cowboy in New Mexico, where, while riding with a herd of cattle, he was killed by lightning.

Now in her fifties, Cecil went to work trying to make a living on her hardscrabble ranch—alone. Life was very difficult, but among the sparse sagebrush, Cecil laid a foundation, built a house and created a sophisticated water system so she wouldn't have to carry water from Clear Creek, which was a half-mile away. And she rustled cattle.

Most ranchers knew Cecil was stealing a cow now and then for food, not for profit, and let the thievery go unpunished. By 1954, a dispute over a boundary with her neighbor escalated, shots were fired and the sheriff was called. When the sheriff explained that he would need for Cecil to go into Winslow with him, she asked if she could go and lock up her house. Shortly after, he heard a shot and immediately realized that Cecil had committed suicide.

The *Arizona Republic* reported that after her death, it was discovered that Cecil had written articles for western magazines under the name of Juanita Mullins and was also a prolific artist who painted with oils. An article written by Bob Thomas and published in *Arizona Highways* in 1995 cited local women who knew Cecil, and all agreed that she was a kind, gentle, fun-loving person who was forced into a life of crime by local ranchers.

Cecil's peers believed the men resented her arrogance and independence, the way she dressed and her unusual skill with a horse, a lariat and a gun. This former Harvey Girl was the first—and most likely the only—female cattle rustler in northern Arizona.

When Harvey Girls and other Harvey employees reminisce about their years with Fred Harvey, invariably, they describe the experience as being part of a large family. The girls helped each other through bouts of being homesick or a romance turned sour. Harmless pranks were frequent, especially when a fresh-faced, naive Harvey Girl–in–training showed up behind the lunch counter. When oysters on the half-shell were on the menu, the new girl would be told by an experienced Harvey Girl that once the oyster dish was cleared from the table, the shells had to be thoroughly washed and saved to be used again. Once the unsuspecting girl began scrubbing an oyster shell, someone would let her in on the joke.

Despite the many rules and measures in place to provide a safe environment for Harvey employees, in the early twentieth century, the West was an unruly territory and often provided a haven for folks with dodgy reputations. It seems, from newspaper accounts of the time, that the most serious violations occurred in the kitchen area, away from those being served in the refined surroundings of the Harvey House.

Local newspapers often recounted instances in which food or money was stolen from a Harvey House. One occurrence in Seligman landed a man and his son in jail for thirty days for stealing potatoes from the Havasu kitchen. In Ash Fork, a disgruntled former Harvey House dishwasher was sentenced to "forty days' imprisonment" for forcibly seating chef Charles Jordan on a "red hot range." Chef Jordan was not seriously injured and "got hold of a butcher knife and chased the offender out of the building." It was also reported that Chef Jordan was able to continue working because his responsibilities could be handled while standing up.

When Fred Harvey decided to handpick waitresses, attire them in proper, starched uniforms and send them out to feed the traveling public, I am not sure he realized how Harvey Girls would change the course of women's history. Yet change it they did!

3

HARVEY GIRLS ON THE SILVER SCREEN

*A*s I chose the title for this chapter, I realized that if you are reading this book and you have seen the 1946 MGM movie *The Harvey Girls*, you probably didn't see it on the large screen at a movie theater. Instead, you most likely enjoyed the delightful musical on a classic movie television channel. However, for the purposes of this book, let's envision how it must have been to watch popular celebrities of the time—Judy Garland, Ray Bolger and Angela Lansbury—in a feisty musical on the big screen while enjoying a bag of popcorn. The movie was based on the book by Samuel Adams and told the story of young, bold women who came west to be Harvey Girls.

When the movie made it to big screens across the country, theatergoers were introduced to the story of the Harvey Girls with these words: "When Fred Harvey pushed his chain of restaurants farther and farther west along the lengthening tracks of the Santa Fe, he brought with him one of the first civilizing forces this land had known: the Harvey Girls. These winsome waitresses conquered the West as surely as David Crockett and the Kit Carsons—not with powder horn and rifle but with a beefsteak and a cup of coffee."

The most memorable song in the movie is "On the Atchison, Topeka and the Santa Fe," with lyrics by Johnny Mercer and music by Harry Warren. In an interview, Mercer explained that he had seen the name of the railroad on a boxcar and thought it had a "nice, lyrical quality to it." After signing to write the music for the Harvey Girl movie, Mercer suggested a song about

Publicity photograph of Judy Garland, one of the stars in the 1946 movie *The Harvey Girls. Courtesy of Michael McMillan.*

the railroad. After he had Warren's music, Mercer said he went to work on the words: "It was an easy one to write. As I recall, it took me about an hour." The song won an Academy Award for Best Song in 1946.

The "train" song continues to be familiar after all this time; however, my favorite Mercer/Warren song in the movie is "The Train Must Be Fed," with lyrics that emphasize the high-level of service expected by Fred Harvey. Garland sings about the perfection of Harvey Girl uniforms, perfection in the dining room and in Harvey Girl living quarters and "perfection in the way we feed the trains." This last line, of course, refers to the passengers who found their way from passenger trains into the trackside Harvey Houses to enjoy a meal served with Fred Harvey perfection.

The conservative, traditional Fred Harvey company was originally opposed to the making of the Harvey Girl movie. Byron Harvey Sr., president of the company at the time, turned away a scout from a major California studio, expressing concerns about how his company and its Harvey Girls might be portrayed on the big screen. Months later, Byron was approached by a representative of Metro-Goldwyn-Mayer (MGM). A draft of a script was provided and met Byron's tentative approval. He was given assurance that the Fred Harvey company would be allowed to approve each phase of the production. The MGM movie scout also brought a musical score and a singer to the Chicago Fred Harvey offices. One version of the story describes the scene: "A delegation of Harveys accompanied the Metro man to a piano at the Blackstone Hotel on Michigan Avenue. There the singing of the score—especially the catchy 'Atchison, Topeka & Santa Fe'—disolved [*sic*] all objections."

Actually, the musical, released over seventy years ago, evolved into an extremely clever Fred Harvey marketing tactic. Ongoing correspondence between MGM Pictures and the Fred Harvey company reveals the strong influence that Harvey executives tried to wield on advance publicity for the movie as well as the movie itself. To help appease the Harvey family, Byron Harvey Jr., grandson of Fred Harvey, was brought to California as a technical adviser and given a cameo role in the movie as a Santa Fe brakeman. A publicity photo was released showing the star of the movie, Judy Garland, with Byron Jr. and Byron Sr. all seated in movie director's chairs.

The Harvey Girls was declared one of the top movies of 1946 based on its gross earnings of $1.2 million ($16.5 million in 2019). The national attention the movie would bring to Harvey Houses would certainly be a boon for business, but the reputation of the Harvey Girls had to be protected. In the fall of 1945, MGM began production of placards and other printed material to promote the January 1946 release of *The Harvey Girls*. Fred Harvey executives were not pleased. An October 1945 telegram from Byron Harvey Sr. to the MGM publicity department complained that the magazine and billboard advertising gave "the erroneous impression that this picture is largely a burlesque show or that the Harvey Girls were dance hall girls. In my opinion this type of advertising not only misrepresents the general character of the picture but is highly damaging to our company and its employees and is directly contrary to the spirit of our understanding."

Byron cited a letter he had written to MGM the previous year when he specified "that the production should be of such high quality that any publicity which the Fred Harvey system may derive from the picture will be of a favorable nature." Byron also stated that he had not seen the movie. "However, I feel very strongly that any favorable publicity our company and its employees may derive from the picture itself will be more than offset by such sensational advertising as is now apparently being produced."

Chief publicist and director of advertising for MGM, Howard Dietz, responded from his New York office: "I have gone over the ads and while we do use the dancing girl motif quite frequently it does not seem to be used offensively and is consistent with the idea of a musical picture." Dietz promised that "wherever possible in material not yet prepared we shall do our best to tone down what you consider objectionable and also attempt to make it clear that the Harvey Girls were not burlesque queens." With a conciliatory note, Dietz concluded: "I shall be extremely uncomfortable if you are dissatisfied with the treatment of the film and I want to do everything I can to find common ground."

Telegrams and letters between the two powerful men continued for some time, with Byron Harvey continuing to press his midwestern sensibilities on the New York publicity mogul. Harvey wrote that he found it "particularly objectionable" that Dietz's posters prominently featured "Alhambra [the saloon in the movie] girls with only minor picturization [*sic*] of Harvey Girls and with the wording 'The Harvey Girls' appearing opposite Angela Lansbury's legs." He went on to call the MGM advertising plan an "exploitation manual" and criticized proposed slogans for newspaper advertising. "If these slogans reflect your people's conception of the Harvey Girls picture I cannot help but feel deeply regretful for having given permission for this production. I hope you can send out one of your responsible assistants to show me other proposed advertising and to explain what steps are being taken to overcome my objections."

Byron Harvey also declined an invitation to come to New York for a screening of *The Harvey Girls* and stated, "I do hope you will decide to arrange a private showing for me in Chicago at an early date, as previously promised by your people in New York and Hollywood."

It may have been difficult for the Fred Harvey company to bring New York and Hollywood up to its standards, but the Fred Harvey home office maintained strict control over how publicity for the movie was handled in its establishments. Rigorous guidelines were provided to Harvey managers concerning promotion of the movie in Harvey Houses. Small posters were provided to all locations, and managers were told to attach them "on the bulletin board in the kitchen or fastened with gummed tape to the wall in a prominent location" so "your entire crew" will see them. The highly coordinated promotional message to the Harvey employees was, in Byron Harvey's words: "Millions are seeing *The Harvey Girls* on the screen and many of them will see us every day. Let's all be at our best!"

Large, freestanding cutouts of Judy Garland in a pristine black-and-white uniform were prominently displayed in Harvey House restaurants in towns where there was also a movie theater screening *The Harvey Girls*. Managers were instructed to acknowledge to the Fred Harvey main office that they received the cardboard figures and told to send an exact description of where the figures would be displayed.

The Harvey company also distributed special menus featuring promotional photos (without saloon girls) from the movie. The menus were sent to Harvey Houses in December 1945, but managers were instructed not to use them too far in advance of the premiere of the movie early the next year. During this time, the Fred Harvey company also ran large ads in magazines with the headline, "What…a movie about us?" Always a marketing machine, Byron Harvey sent a reminder to managers: "In order for us to reap the potential benefits from this motion picture, it is necessary for us to have our house in order—standards of service, food, cleanliness, courtesy, and personnel at the very highest peak. We realize all this comes to us at a time when [we] are still very busy with the many problems left over from the war. Nevertheless we should grasp this opportunity and make the most of it. I am counting on all of you to do your very best to this end." The Fred Harvey company was doing business, over forty years later, in the same way that Fred Harvey—the man—had before his death. And, as originally intended, the attention to detail and service was a major windfall to train travel from Kansas to California as thousands traveled by rail knowing that Fred Harvey would take care of them.

Real Harvey Girls didn't sing and dance as much as Judy Garland did in the 1946 movie, but they worked hard, had some fun along the way and made Fred Harvey proud. All these decades later, we are proud, too, and thankful that thousands of women took a path away from familiarity and made life better for folks across northern Arizona.

4
HOSPITALITY DONE RIGHT

*A*rizona offered many attractive experiences for a growing tourist business, and the Fred Harvey company recognized the potential for luxury hotels along the Santa Fe railway that stretched across the northern part of the state. By this time, train passengers knew they would enjoy delicious, freshly prepared meals in the now-famous Harvey restaurants, and many were eager to stop and stay awhile in a Harvey hotel.

ASH FORK: ESCALANTE (1906–1948)

Ash Fork's first Harvey House was a two-story wood-frame building built around 1895. In 1905, a fire started in the Harvey House kitchen, and because there was no firefighting equipment available, the Harvey House and railroad depot were completely destroyed. The Ash Fork Harvey staff was temporarily put to work at the Seligman, Arizona Harvey House. Immediately following this disaster, Santa Fe officials announced that the company would spend $640,000 during the coming year to improve the railroad line and equipment between Albuquerque, New Mexico, and Ash Fork. Of this money, $75,000 was earmarked for a new depot and Harvey House in Ash Fork.

During a brief train stop in Flagstaff, Ford Harvey was interviewed by the *Coconino Sun*. The newspaper reported that while there, "Mr. Harvey was a

An artist's rendering of the Escalante in Ash Fork, Arizona. Construction costs for the reinforced concrete Harvey hotel exceeded $100,000. *Courtesy of Tom Taylor.*

very busy man and transacted a large amount of business. He declared that the 'new house' planned for Ash Fork would be built 'with an eye to comfort and will be one of the best appointed houses on the line of the Santa Fe. We intend to make it a very pretty and handsomely furnished hotel.'"

As with any large construction job, the Escalante project did not always go smoothly. In addition to a considerable overage on the cost of the building, there was considerable controversy over a change in location of approximately five hundred feet from the site of the original Harvey House and depot. This was not well accepted by local residents and businessmen who believed this would be too great a distance from the business district of town. The close proximity of the original Harvey House and depot assured traffic to local businesses from train passengers.

Construction on the Escalante had just begun when trouble broke out. An incident reported under the headline "Mexicans and Japs Fight at Ash Fork" in the *Arizona Republic* caused considerable concern among residents. Approximately forty "natives of Spanish extraction" who were working on dirt excavation for the Escalante were attacked by approximately sixty "natives of the Chrysanthemum Isle employed as section hands on the main line of the Santa Fe Pacific railroad, armed with picks and shovels." Apparently, "the fight was the outcome of some petty quarrels and differences between the plucky Japs and the descendants of the Spanish cavaliers." Three of the attackers were badly injured, and "but for the timely interference of the railroad timekeeper, who is a native American, who spoke word of peace from behind a double barrel shotgun, it is probable that some lives would have been lost in the encounter." Early the next day, over half of "the belligerent Japs resigned and left for the raisin fields of the Golden state."

Perhaps this type of disorder precipitated the use of guards to protect young women when they arrived in Ash Fork to staff the new Harvey House. Newspaper stories reported that "the women were brought in under heavy guard to protect them from lumbermen, miners and railroad workers who lived in the territory."

The initial cost estimate for the luxurious Escalante missed the mark by $40,000. The Harvey compound opened to the public in 1907 at a final cost of $115,000. Named for the eighteenth-century Spanish explorer Silvestre Escalante, who journeyed into Arizona in 1776, the newest Fred Harvey hotel also had a Harvey House lunchroom with adjacent newsstand, a large dining room (thirty-seven by sixty-five feet), a curio shop with Native American arts and crafts and a barbershop.

The building also housed a large cold storage area and an electric light plant. Constructed of reinforced concrete, the two-story building featured an expansive open balcony across the front that spanned more than four hundred feet. A covered screened porch stretched across the back of the building. The Escalante was connected to the railroad depot by an arcade and surrounded by desert flowers, fountains and a large cactus garden and was advertised as the best Harvey House west of Chicago. Fifty-four guest rooms on the second floor offered conveniences such as telephones, hot and cold running water, electric lights, private baths and steam heat. Some of these rooms were home to the Harvey Girls who "fed the trains" in Ash Fork twenty-four hours a day, seven days a week. A few days before the anticipated opening of this newest Harvey House, fourteen railcars containing furniture, fixtures and "other trimmings" were on the side tracks in Ash Fork.

The Escalante served as a hub for a flourishing tourism industry and housed railroad men during layovers. It also became the center of the town's social life, hosting many banquets, parties and masquerade balls. One of the Harvey managers, Mr. Degardo, introduced a new dance known as the Harvey House shuffle that was a favorite of guests and off-duty Harvey employees.

The once elegant hotel closed in 1948, and two years later, the restaurant ceased operations. Although Ash Fork residents tried to save the stately

The curio shop at the Escalante offered a large display of Native American arts and crafts for sale. *Courtesy of Tom Taylor.*

The large dining room at the Escalante Harvey House in Ash Fork, Arizona, with tables set with customary Fred Harvey linens, silver, crystal and china. *Courtesy of Tom Taylor.*

building, the Escalante was demolished in 1968. The Ash Fork Historical Society Museum preserves the local Harvey and railroad history and features a quarter-inch scale model of the Escalante built by Ash Fork residents Wayne and Nancy Ulrich.

Although given the name Hattie Bea when she was born, Dixie Hudson spent most of her adult life correcting others to call her Dixie, a name she felt more characterized her spirit and energy. Dixie graduated from high school in her hometown of Huntsville, Missouri, and immediately left for Ash Fork, Arizona, to work as a Harvey Girl. Within a year, at age nineteen, her high-spirited personality caught the attention of Frank Cassity, a twenty-six-year-old accountant for the Fred Harvey company, and they soon married. The couple left Harvey employment, moved to Los Angeles and later retired in Reno, Nevada.

Cora Mathis Scott grew up in Wisconsin and, having been told by her father that she could not leave home until her eighteenth birthday, set out the day after for Ash Fork, Arizona. Her sister was already working at the Escalante Hotel, so with her sister's recommendation, Cora was immediately hired. Following a week of training, Cora went to work in the lunchroom. In an oral history interview, Cora explained that being a Harvey Girl was hard work. "You didn't walk, you ran." She enjoyed living in the dormitory with the other Harvey Girls and "enjoyed meeting new people. It was different, you know and the cowboys…they were real cowboys then. They weren't those that go around dressing like them. They were really working with the cows!" After seven months at the Escalante, Cora moved to San Diego to attend nursing school.

Every Harvey House had as many Harvey "guys" as Harvey Girls to keep everything running smoothly. The kitchen was almost always staffed with men—a chef (often from Europe), a salad boy, a vegetable boy, bakers and an ice cream boy, along with dishwashers and other cleaning staff. Numerous men also staffed the Harvey hotels located adjacent to the Harvey restaurants. In 1950, the *Arizona Republic* printed the story of one of these men who had a long career as a "bellboy" at the Escalante. The article credited "Harvey boys" with filling a less glamorous—albeit equally important—role in providing exemplary Harvey service to travelers in Arizona.

George "Chico" Shiga completed over forty-two years of service at the Escalante in 1950 at the age of seventy-three. Shiga was born in Shukoshima, Japan, and "his first job, three years before the first Harvey hotels opened four thousand miles away, was setting type in a newspaper office." The young man had a desire to see the world and took a job as a cabin boy on a

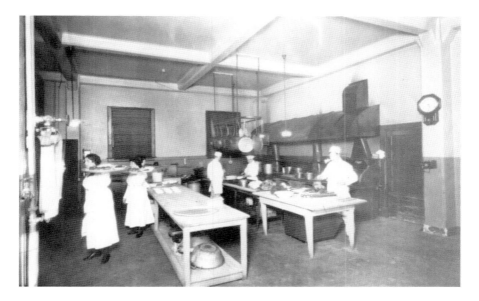

A typical Fred Harvey kitchen at the Escalante with a crew of Harvey "guys" preparing food for hundreds of diners each day. *Courtesy of Special Collections, University of Arizona Libraries, Fred Harvey collection (AZ 326).*

ship traveling to the Dutch East Indies, China and Honolulu before landing in Los Angeles. At this point in his travels, Shiga remembers that he had no money, no job and was unable to speak English. How he came upon the information that there was a porter's job open at the new Harvey House in Ash Fork remains a mystery; however, George was hired, and this became his first and last job in the United States.

At the time Shiga began his Harvey career in 1908, the population of Ash Fork had reached almost 500. The census of the time shows the majority of residents were classified as white, 101 were Hispanics, 2 were African Americans, 6 were Chinese and 12 were Japanese (11 of whom worked at the Harvey House).

Shiga remembers well the early days "when some cowpunchers rode into Ash Fork, hitched their horses to the downtown post and tiptoed along the cement walk to the Harvey House in order not to roll their spurs." Not all cowboys were this respectful, and many came to town "going up and down the streets shooting at random and driving townspeople indoors for protection." Shiga says that "mysterious killings were the order of the day. There was hardly a morning without least one victim lying in the streets. Man dead…no good no more."

When the original Harvey hotel in Ash Fork burned down, Shiga, now known as Chico to coworkers and customers, worked for Fred Harvey in Seligman, Arizona, doing odd jobs on the Harvey farm. He was very happy to return to his job at the new Escalante! Shiga remembers the first automobile that came down the hill from Williams. "It was a Pierce-Arrow all covered with brass" and made the trip from Williams to Ash Fork in four hours over mud roads. Outside of Ash Fork, the car got stuck and had to be pulled out by a mule team.

During Shiga's early years, there were no laws regulating work hours. He would begin his day at 7:00 a.m. and work late into the night. Once, he received a ten-dollar tip from a grateful customer and tried to return it because he felt he hadn't done anything to earn it, telling the customer, "A dollar is plenty." During one four-year period, the diminutive, courteous Harvey employee polished the shoes of visiting dignitaries during the daytime hours, and at five in the morning, he would clean the bar of the leftovers from the previous night's revelries. In later years, Shiga worked as a bellboy and a housekeeper.

Still speaking in broken English, Shiga related the circumstances that led to him losing one of his prized possessions—a camera. "During the last war, when all Japanese were under close observation, my camera, knife

Colorful rugs and pottery decorated the lobby of the Escalante in Ash Fork, Arizona. *Courtesy of Tom Taylor.*

and several other personal possessions were taken by FBI men." However, Shiga was never questioned or detained. The Fred Harvey company didn't offer a retirement plan for its employees; however, Chico wasn't worried. He had purchased savings bonds with most of his earnings, and using those funds (along with the free train pass awarded to him by the Harvey company upon retirement), George "Chico" Shiga had plans to travel to Phoenix, Arizona—the first destination on his list.

Harvey Girl historian Brenda Thowe shared a story about another Harvey guy and dear friend of hers, Arthur Sandoval. "Arthur is my most memorable and favorite Harvey guy. He was a salad maker at the Harvey House in Winslow. Arthur would show me how he whipped the dressing for the salad by tying the bowl with a towel around his waist. He would beat with one hand and mix in more ingredients with the other. Everything was fresh, and if you stopped beating, the dressing would separate and you would have to start over again." Arthur later was hired by the Santa Fe to work on track gangs and worked his way up to foreman of the gang. Surely, before leaving the Harvey House, Arthur passed his creative technique for making salad dressing to other kitchen staff.

SELIGMAN: THE HAVASU (1913–1948)

The first wood-frame Harvey House at Seligman (originally called Prescott Junction), located twenty-two miles west of Ash Fork, opened in 1895. Ten years later, the two-story, sixty-thousand-square-foot Havasu began hosting travelers and locals in typical Fred Harvey fashion. With an exterior of half-timbers against stucco, this impressive trackside hotel was named after the native Havasupai tribe. The Prairie-style Havasu had guest rooms, a lunch counter with seating for forty-seven and a dining room that served eighty. The Havasu closed in 1954, and the building was demolished in 2008.

An unidentified train passenger on the Santa Fe No. 10 during the early 1900s wrote in the *Santa Fe Employes' [sic] Magazine* the following description of a situation he encountered in Seligman. "We left Los Angeles on July 27, and we pulled into Seligman on July 28 at 4:10 p.m., on time. It had been raining exceptionally heavily the greater part of the afternoon, and some of us were not very much surprised when a washout was announced at Crookton, nine miles east of Seligman. It was supposed that we would continue eastward before midnight, but the continued heavy rains in the

The sixty-thousand-square-foot Seligman, Arizona Harvey House was named Havasu after the native Havasupai tribe of the area. *Courtesy of Michael McMillan.*

The lunch counter at the Havasu in Seligman, Arizona. *Courtesy of Special Collections, University of Arizona Libraries, Fred Harvey collection (AZ 326).*

mountains caused the water to flow over the wash and delayed operations. The regular Friday evening dance given by the Seligman boys at the reading room was announced for Thursday when it was found that we were to be their guests for that night. Supper was served at the Harvey House." The next day, train travel was still impossible, and the Harvey staff arranged a trip for the stranded passengers to visit the "Indian village, the canyon and the bottomless pit." However, before a flatcar could be readied and hitched to the railyard "goat" for the day's adventure, the rains began again. The next day, the rain had subsided, the washout had been repaired and the passengers on No. 10 were on their way again. "During all the time of our enforced stay at this hospitable railroad town of Seligman we were kept well entertained. The Harvey House served meals free of charge to those delayed. There was not one murmur of dissent, not one word of complaint uttered by the passengers. I speak for all of them in words of praise for all those who so unselfishly and so thoroughly entertained us."

The Fred Harvey staff at the Havasu in 1938. The two men in white in the center of the front row are chefs in the Havasu kitchen. *Courtesy of Arizona State Library, Archives and Public Records, History and Archives Division, Phoenix, No. 01-4706.*

Best friends and Harvey Girls Tillie Raugh (*left*) and Clara Stork Greenlaw (*right*) in front of the Santa Fe Reading Room in Seligman, Arizona. *Courtesy of Don Gray.*

Clara Stork's grandson, Don Gray, told me the true story of two Wisconsin girls who came west: "Clara and Tillie [Matilda Raugh] were friends in Wausau, Wisconsin, as they grew up. At about the age of 17 [in 1909], they heard about the Harvey Houses and talked to their parents to get permission to go to work." Most likely the first Harvey House where the girls worked was at the Cardenas in Trinidad, Colorado. "They also worked at the Alvarado in Albuquerque, New Mexico, before ending up at the Havasu in Seligman, Arizona."

Charles A. Greenlaw Jr. was a Seligman businessman who often dined at the lunch counter at the Havasu, and it was there that he and Clara met. The couple married on January 1, 1917, on the Greenlaw Ranch in East Flagstaff.

Tillie continued to work for Fred Harvey and moved to the Escalante in Ash Fork, where she was given the responsibilities of head lunch girl. In 1923, Tillie left her career with Fred Harvey and moved back to Wisconsin to help care for her mother. There, she worked as a waitress and hostess for the Milwaukee Road Railroad and was instrumental in the formation of the Milwaukee Railroad Credit Union. Tillie was recognized on the occasion of her ninetieth birthday in 1984 for "assisting elderly shut-ins with their banking and other business affairs." She never married and passed away in 1987. Tillie and Clara remained lifelong friends.

Harvey Girl Luz Delgadillo grew up in Seligman during the 1930s, and although her dream was to become a Naval WAVE (Women Accepted for Volunteer Emergency Service) or join the WAC (Women's Army Corps) during World War II, she couldn't go against the wishes of her parents. Instead, she stayed in Seligman and, as a Harvey Girl at the Havasu, helped serve thousands of soldiers as they traveled by train to the Pacific coast.

Luz and her family were well known in the small Arizona railroad town and throughout northern Arizona. Her father, Angel, was instrumental in persuading the State of Arizona to designate Route 66 a historic highway and helped with the founding of the Historic Route 66 Association of Arizona. Luz and six of her brothers comprised the Delgadillo Orchestra. The group traveled to gigs along Route 66 in Williams, Ash Fork, Flagstaff and Winslow for over thirty years.

"I was a beautician in Dallas after graduating from high school in Cranfills Gap, Texas," Frances Hansen Coffey said. "It was during the Depression, and I couldn't make a living. My parents kept sending me money, and I thought, 'This is not good.'" A cousin told Frances about her work for Fred Harvey in Ash Fork, Arizona, and Frances decided to apply. She began as a Harvey Girl in Kingman and then transferred to Seligman in 1937.

Harvey Girl Frances Hansen Coffey with an unidentified friend in front of the Havasu in Seligman in 1937. *Courtesy of Arizona State Library, Archives and Public Records, History and Archives Division, Phoenix, No. 01-4703.*

At least fourteen to sixteen passenger trains, eastbound and westbound, arrived every day in Seligman. Waitresses served, cleaned up and reset places every thirty to forty minutes. "It was hard work, but it was fun also," Frances said. "On our days off, one of our favorite pastimes was to go outside of town, where big cattle drives were being held awaiting shipment. We ate the evening meal at the chuck wagon and sang along with the cowboys." During one of these evenings, Frances met Sam Coffey, who had come to Arizona from Tarpley, Texas. Within a year, they married, and Sam left his cowboy days behind and went to work for the Santa Fe, eventually becoming an engineer.

WILLIAMS: FRAY MARCOS (1908–1954)

Often, the first Santa Fe and Fred Harvey buildings in small railroad towns were railroad boxcars—a far cry from the thoughtfully designed permanent buildings that followed. In Williams, a town referred to as the gateway to the Grand Canyon, the depot was originally a boxcar, and the first Harvey restaurant opened in 1894 in a substandard building previously occupied by another restaurant that had been operating for several years.

Certainly, any railroad town welcomed a Harvey House, and if a hotel were part of the package, it was even better. A Harvey House brought with it the promise of passengers leaving the train and spreading into the local business district when the train made a stop for fuel. However, there were also challenges from locals as the Harvey system attempted to embed itself into local culture. The *Williams News* (hyped as "the newsy and reliable paper" of northern Arizona) printed this page-two notice in 1904: "The Harvey House management would do well to have their cess pool [*sic*] cleaned at night instead of in the middle of the day. To have to breathe bad air is not wholesome at any time but as long as we have to take it we would prefer the night when most of us are asleep and would be unconscious of it."

During the early planning stages, in 1905, Ford Harvey described the new Harvey hotel in Williams as a "neat but small hotel for the accommodation of our Grand Canyon trade and the local business. It will be a small house, but will be modern and its furnishings will be up to the standard of the system." In addition to the construction of a hotel, plans were in place to enlarge the Santa Fe depot in Williams and build a six-stall roundhouse for servicing and storing locomotives.

An artist's rendering of Fray Marcos in Williams, Arizona. *Courtesy of Tom Taylor.*

Increased travel to the Grand Canyon in the summer during this time period prompted an increase in regular train runs from Williams as well as special cars and trains of tourists. Of course, the astute Ford Harvey recognized that perhaps this situation called for a larger Harvey House. Two years later, it was announced that the Williams "Harvey eating house would be one of the largest and finest among the hotels recently built by the company," and the locomotive roundhouse would have eight stalls. Indeed, when the contract for the new Harvey hotel was issued, the structure would include a curio room, a newsstand, lunch and dining rooms, a kitchen with appropriate pantry and cold storage attached and a laundry, as well as thirty-five guest rooms.

At 11:00 a.m. on Tuesday, March 10, 1908, train No. 1 rolled into Williams, bringing the first passengers that would enter the new Fray Marcos hotel. Among those passengers were Santa Fe Railway dignitaries and J.F. Huckel, general manager of the Harvey system. A large number of prominent local citizens enjoyed supper at the hotel that evening, and the *Williams News* enumerated the advantages of having this Harvey hotel in their town, although it was acknowledged that "the Harvey people will not spend a great deal of money here"—referring to the fact that for a hotel and restaurant of this size, food supplies would not be purchased locally but shipped in from Harvey farms and ranches. However, Fray Marcos was seen as "a valuable feature for the town of Williams from an advertising standpoint and thousands of visitors who will come here in the future will receive a more favorable impression of our town because the Fray Marcos is here to greet them and afford them all the comforts, conveniences and luxuries to be had in a large city." Two years after it opened, the hotel employed up to fifty people with an average monthly payroll of $2,000 for the entire staff.

As with all new Harvey hotels, the two-story, mission-style building was steam-heated and lit by electricity. Fray Marcos was advertised as "practically fire proof," yet "fire-fighting contrivances have been judiciously installed." The large curio room, also known as the Indian room, managed by J.B. Canfield, was described as "well lighted and luxuriously furnished" and containing "everything in the curio line that is to be had." The name of the hotel was in honor of the Spanish Franciscan missionary Fray Marcos de Niza, celebrated by many as the first "white pioneer" to enter Arizona.

Around Christmastime, residents of Williams—as well as those traveling through—were treated to the elaborate, festive decorations that adorned Fray Marcos. Mrs. Louis DeBold, the wife of the Fray Marcos manager, would spend an entire day in the Indian room behind locked doors decorating several Christmas trees placed throughout the Harvey House. One particular tree for Christmas 1919 was dubbed by the *Williams News* as the most attractive in town. It was "heavily, but tastily laden with gold and silver tinsel, glittering balls and candles," while other holiday decorations were typically evergreens with red bows. The Christmas dinner menu offered at Fray Marcos was as delightful as the decorations. The meal began with a choice of "Blue Points on Half Shell, Gumbo ala Creo'le, Connsome en Tasse, celery and ripe olives." The main course offered "Columbia River Salmon Normande, Frog Saddles Tartar Sauce, Sweet Breads Braised au Champignons, Roast Young Turkey with Oyster Dressing and Cranberry Sauce or Roast Prime Ribs of Beef au Jus." Side dishes were "Potatoes Parisienne, Crushed Turnips, Candied Yams, Mashed Potatoes, Cauliflower in Cream." All diners were offered "Punch Benedictine," made with a French herbal liqueur, or tea or coffee. Dessert was traditional "Mince Pie, Pumpkin Pie or English Plum Pudding with Brandy Sauce." Depending on a diner's choices, the meal would cost between $2.25 and $2.75.

Mrs. DeBold was often mentioned in the "social notes" of the local newspaper, the *Williams News*, as the hostess of community events, and her decorating flare left its mark on the town. Often, in addition to details about the room and table decorations she created, Mrs. DeBold's attire was noted, such as the dress she wore to a farewell dinner for a young lady who was going to Los Angeles for the winter: "The ladies were in full evening apparel, especially noticeable was the gown of the hostess [Mrs. DeBold], a black charmeuse with an overdress of chiffon embroidered in silver. A single red, red rose at the corsage was the only ornament." It was noted that the guest of honor wore a "girlish gown of white crepe de chine." At the end of the evening, "the guests departed voting Mrs. DeBold a most delightful hostess." Mr. and Mrs. DeBold worked for Fred Harvey for many years in Texas, Kansas, California and Arizona.

The hotel business in Williams was booming, and the Harvey company realized that "the accommodations of this hotel were altogether too inadequate for the large and ever growing tourist business." A year after Fray Marcos opened, the Harvey company announced an investment of $35,000 to construct a thirty-room addition to the hotel.

In 1923, twenty-two more guest rooms were added to the original hotel building, and Fray Marcos continued to efficiently serve travelers and locals until it closed thirty-one years later. The Williams Elks Lodge leased the abandoned building from Santa Fe Railway in 1963 and, for a time, used the former Harvey House for the organization's activities and rented it to other organizations.

Mary Duffy was only fifteen when, in 1891, she left Ireland with her mother, sister and brother to join her father, who had been working in the copper-mining town of Bagdad, Arizona. "The 'west fever' had lured my father away from Ireland," Mary said in a 1957 newspaper interview. "When we arrived we'd been seasick 11 days on the water before we took the long train trip and Mother was worn out. But when we got to Williams and she saw Indians lounging around the box-car depot, she was so terrified that my father had to drag her off the train." Recovering from the initial shock, Mary's mother "settled happily into the friendly little town of Williams."

Unfortunately, within a short time, Mary's father died, and to help support her mother and siblings, Mary joined the ranks of the Harvey Girls in the original Williams Harvey House. At this time, Santa Fe employees and carpenters who were building the Santa Fe section houses were the primary diners rather than train passengers. "My recreation time was spent dancing whenever I got the chance," Mary said. "I would promise the porter I would do part of his work the next day, if he would clear my tables for me so I could leave in time for the dance. We would travel great distances by wagon over terrible roads to get to a dance. And then we would dance until daylight and I would get back just in time to put on my uniform and go to work."

A bedroom with bathroom en suite in the Fray Marcos Fred Harvey hotel. *Courtesy of Special Collections, University of Arizona Libraries, Fred Harvey collection (AZ 326).*

No doubt Mary's vivacious personality, piercing blue eyes and lilting Irish brogue made her a popular partner on the dance floor!

An elegant Harvey hotel—with amenities—was a bright spot in Williams, but it couldn't entirely change the nature of the early town even into the twentieth century. Kathryn Massey, who worked as a Harvey Girl at Fray Marcos in 1928, remembered receiving a couple of significant warnings upon her arrival in Williams. Harvey Girls were not to be seen in the downtown vicinity of the town that was dominated by "houses of ill-repute," or they would be released from their duties. And a waitress would receive a reprimand if she dated the "wrong man," meaning if he wasn't up to Harvey standards. In some locations, if a Harvey Girl wanted to go out with a young man, she was required to have him meet the manager, who had to approve of the boy.

After a personal interview with Alice Steele in the Fred Harvey Kansas City office, Nellie Berg Veley was uncertain about her future as a Harvey Girl. In 1937, after graduating from high school in St. Ansgar, Iowa, Nellie was visiting with an aunt in Kansas City and heard that Fred Harvey was hiring

The inviting lobby of the Fray Marcos hotel in Williams, Arizona, was a favorite meeting place for train passengers as well as locals. *Courtesy of Tom Taylor.*

A large stone fireplace in the Indian room of Fray Marcos captured the attention of visitors coming into the main entrance to the hotel. *Courtesy of Tom Taylor.*

again. Nellie's older sister, Olga, had already been hired as a Harvey Girl and was working in Belen, New Mexico. "I was scared and Miss Steele knew it. She was so kind!" The seventeen-year-old was asked if she had experience as a waitress and whether she liked people. "I was truthful about not having waitressing experience, but I lied about my age." The age requirement for a Harvey Girl was eighteen.

Nellie returned home, and according to her daughter, Kay Roth, "Mom didn't think a whole lot of it until about three weeks later, when she got a crisp white envelope with the Fred Harvey logo embossed on it. Inside the envelope was the offer of a job, a six-month contract and a train pass to Vaughn, New Mexico."

After Nellie completed her training in Vaughn, she was sent to work in Belen, New Mexico, after that Harvey House reopened to serve the troop trains. Now a seasoned Harvey Girl, Nellie worked at the Alvarado in Albuquerque, New Mexico, and was later sent to Fray Marcos. From there, Nellie was often dispatched to El Tovar in the Grand Canyon and La Fonda in Santa Fe, New Mexico, on special assignments. Nellie remembered that regardless of where she worked, requirements were strict and included always wearing a girdle and a hairnet. "Our white skirts, blouses, shoes and stockings had to be spotless. They even checked our fingernails." If a Harvey Girl violated a Harvey rule, she was usually given a second chance. "The managers were quite liberal because they liked to keep the girls that did good work." During the war, it became impossible to get white hose, and Harvey Girls were allowed to wear regular hose. But those soon became a precious commodity as well.

"When I was working in Williams, two well-dressed women would come into the lunch room regularly," Nellie recalled in a letter to the author. "The older Harvey Girls always had us younger girls wait on them which was fine with us because the women always tipped us five dollars each. In those days a half-dollar tip was unusual and a five dollar tip unheard of!" Later, the young girls learned that the women were prostitutes and thus shunned by the seasoned Harvey Girls. "It didn't matter much to us as we were too green and didn't know enough about sex to really understand. I think the women appreciated the respect we showed them, as we would any customer, because the women gave us gifts at Christmas."

Nellie was in Williams when Pearl Harbor was bombed. In writing the family history, Kay Roth tells that "Mr. Hatfield, the big boss from Chicago, told the girls to open up the dining room and any other space they could

The dining room at Fray Marcos featured elaborate stenciled patterns on the walls and ceilings. *Courtesy of Tom Taylor.*

find for the troop train which was due to arrive. A big party was held for the troops and 500 servicemen were treated to a special time."

WINSLOW: LA POSADA (1930–1957)

The first Winslow Harvey House opened in 1887, but the two-story brick and sandstone building burned down in 1914. Another, larger structure was soon built—with little interruption in the famous Harvey service to train passengers.

After La Posada opened in 1930, the second floor of the previous Harvey House building was used as a dormitory for Harvey Girls, and Santa Fe Railroad offices were on the ground floor. When Verna Welsh came to Winslow to work and first saw the dormitory, she was bewildered. "Everything was covered in red dust and there was only a bed with a mattress, a dresser and a chair. There were no closets and we had to provide our own curtains and bed covers to make the rooms more attractive." In later years, the building was used for Santa Fe division offices; it was torn down in the mid-1960s.

The luxurious La Posada, built on the opposite side of the tracks from the original Harvey House, would be the last of the elegant Harvey hotels. The name is Spanish for "resting place," and the architectural style was that of a leisurely Spanish hacienda with seventy guest rooms and suites. With the legendary imprint and attention to detail of Fred Harvey architect and designer Mary Colter, La Posada was truly an oasis in the desert. Historian Richard Melzer gives credit to Colter for the elegant Spanish arches, sweeping corridors and the inviting furniture in the hotel. "Even new furniture was made to look antique by craftsmen working in an on-site wood shop. With her usual attention to detail, Colter covered guest room floors with Navajo rugs trampled on by construction workers to make the floor coverings look old and used."

In its heyday, the rich and famous from all walks of life flew into Winslow, landing at the largest commercial airport in Arizona and staying a while at La Posada before boarding the train to the West Coast or east to Chicago. Of course, they enjoyed the delicious meals served in the large lunchroom and dining room. No doubt many enjoyed refreshments in the Bull Ring Bar, also a favorite of Winslow locals. Photos in the Fred Harvey employees' magazine, *Hospitality*, show "a lot of people and a lot of gaiety per square foot" at the opening night of the Bull Ring Bar in 1950. Most likely, the guests were served ninety-proof Fred Harvey Special Selection Gin that was back on the market after the wartime ban on distillation. The gin was marketed as "flavored to produce a perfect blend when combined with vermouth or fruit

The early Harvey House in Winslow, Arizona, was later used as a dormitory for Harvey Girls. *Courtesy of Tom Taylor.*

Harvey House staff in Winslow, Arizona, in 1910. *Courtesy of Arizona State Library, Archives and Public Records, History and Archives Division, Phoenix, No. 01-4724.*

La Posada in Winslow, Arizona, was the last Fred Harvey hotel built. It opened in 1930, closed in 1957 and, after restoration, is now once again welcoming guests. *Courtesy of Tom Taylor.*

Lobby of the Winslow, Arizona Harvey House with a Fred Harvey newsstand in the corner. *Courtesy of Tom Taylor.*

The La Posada dining room in Winslow, Arizona, reflected the style of a leisurely Spanish hacienda. *Courtesy of Tom Taylor.*

juices for mixed drinks." Now, for the first time since 1942, every martini mixed in a Harvey cocktail lounge would taste the same. The Fred Harvey gin was bottled "according to a special formula to give our mixed drinks absolute uniformity."

Elizabeth G. Hofflin designed the new cocktail lounge and costumes for the bar hostesses. The costumes were made by Valeria Bernadt, La Posada housekeeper. Draperies in the lounge area were made of "soft yellow spun glass," and the area was furnished with "Pompeian green metal garden furniture upholstered in rose." The phosphorescent tabletops glowed when spotlighted and the floor was covered in chartreuse linoleum "to complete the pastel symphony." The walls were decorated with posters from a bullfight arena in Mexico City. (When I found this description, I couldn't help but wonder whether Mary Colter, original designer of La Posada, ever saw this lounge area. It couldn't have been a more drastic departure from her overall Spanish hacienda design for the hotel.)

Train passengers who chose to stay a while at La Posada often joined an Indian Detour and rode in a Harveycar or Harveycoach—with seating capacities of sixteen and twenty-six, respectively—to Meteor Crater, the Painted Desert Inn, the Petrified Forest and Indian pueblos. These excursions were also popular entertainment for guests at El Tovar in the Grand Canyon.

The Indian Detours were accompanied by guides, called couriers, who were young women—usually natives of Arizona or New Mexico with knowledge of Spanish. Many were college graduates. The couriers, as well as drivers, for the Indian Detours were chosen and trained by an advisory board of nationally recognized authorities on the archaeology, ethnology and history of the Southwest. Drivers were expected to behave like gentlemen and also have extensive mechanical and driving skills. Treacherous roads and heavy demand on the vehicles could present problems for the tours. One Harvey employee remembers that, at one time, the Fred Harvey company used homing pigeons to send word back to home base when a vehicle had broken down.

When the tour group stopped for lunch, their table might be a flat rock, but the food was Harvey House food packed in leather chests. This dining experience was the most persuasive selling point of the tours, for although there were other similar tours available, none were as popular as the Harvey Indian Detours.

A job with the Harveycar Courier Corps offered attractive benefits; the starting salary for the young women was $150 per month, and there was the ever-present opportunity to meet eligible young men! Unfortunately,

The La Posada lunch counters featured decorative Mexican tile not found in other Harvey Houses. *Courtesy of Special Collections, University of Arizona Libraries, Fred Harvey collection (AZ 326).*

with the demise of train travel, there were fewer travelers taking advantage of these specialized "detours," and the Indian Detours ended in 1931 after only five years.

The La Posada closed as a hotel in 1957, and the elegant furnishings were auctioned off. Portions of the building served as the Albuquerque Division Headquarters of the Santa Fe Railroad from the mid-1960s until the late 1980s.

In 1994, seeing the landmark Harvey hotel structure as an "extraordinary treasure," Allan Affeldt and his wife, Tina Mion, began negotiations to purchase the defunct La Posada from the railroad. Embracing Mary Colter's original vision for the design and enlisting the help of business partner Dan Lutzick, the couple moved into La Posada in 1997 and began the restoration.

Today, visitors to a fully restored La Posada stay in comfortable, thoughtfully appointed rooms named for luminaries who stayed at the hotel. Visitors and locals alike enjoy regional contemporary Southwestern cuisine in the Turquoise Room in the space originally occupied by the original

Harveycoaches wait to take El Tovar guests at the Grand Canyon on Indian Detour excursions. *Courtesy of Michael McMillan.*

Fred Harvey restaurant. Adjacent to La Posada grounds, in the historic railroad depot, the Winslow Arts Trust Museum is under construction and is scheduled for completion in 2019. The space was developed by the Winslow Arts Trust, a nonprofit organization dedicated to creating exhibits and programs that celebrate the culture of Winslow and the Route 66 corridor.

Indeed, the beautiful La Posada hotel building, with its thoughtful interior and plush gardens, was a showpiece of the Harvey system; however, the panorama from the hotel looking west toward the tracks was matchless and remains so today. The complete package of present-day La Posada vividly characterizes the romance of train travel. Visit http://laposada.org to learn more about the restored hotel.

As many as seven trains per day stopped at La Posada in the early 1940s. Each train carried up to four hundred passengers. "It was quite an experience to serve people in just thirty minutes," said Verna Northcutt Welsh in a newspaper interview. "We were to set the plates down carefully on the left and clear them afterwards from the customer's right." The experienced Harvey Girl began her career in Newton, Kansas, in the summer of 1937. She then worked for a few years as a secretary with the Kansas state government before coming to Winslow to work with the Harvey manager who had hired her in Kansas, Ray Wright. Verna had expected to work on the hotel desk and

The original mural that embellishes the wall above an archway at La Posada is only one example of the artistic detail throughout the hotel. *Courtesy of Kathy Weir.*

was very disappointed to learn the only job available to her was waitress. "I had no choice because I didn't have train fare to go home…. I worked eight hours a day mostly in the coffee shop and at the lunch counters. We earned twenty-five dollars a month plus our room and board." Verna remembered that their housemother followed the Fred Harvey rules. "Young men were not allowed in the girls' living area. When L.D. [her soon-to-be husband] wanted to see me, he threw rocks at my window."

In 1919, at age twenty-three, Sue Hagood traveled from Davis, Missouri, to the Fred Harvey office in Chicago and, after a rigorous personal interview, was hired to join the ranks of thousands of young women as a Harvey Girl. "A woman checked our backgrounds, trained us there for two weeks without pay and then sent us to our assignments. I wanted to see more of the West," Sue explained. She began work at the Havasu in Seligman, Arizona, and transferred to La Posada in Winslow a year later. Often, Sue worked the early breakfast shift and the evening dinner shift in the same day and had to have a clean uniform for each turn. At this time, Harvey Girls bought their own uniforms, but laundry service was provided at a Harvey laundry facility.

Sue thought her work in the Arizona Harvey Houses was interesting primarily because she enjoyed meeting the passengers from the trains as well as buses from the Painted Desert and Indian Reservation tours. "Many guests stayed overnight after a tour and caught the next day's train. Several times, the dust storms were so bad we couldn't see the trains from the La Posada windows." Sue met William Wetzel on a blind date. "We took long walks north of town to La Prade's dairy. I thought we'd never get out there." Sue and William married in 1932. William obtained their marriage license in Flagstaff, so the wedding party and guests had to go west of Winslow—just past the Coconino County line—so the marriage would be legal.

Over and over again, a Harvey House would be the meeting point for two disparate individuals who would decide to try to make a life together. Such is the story of Irene Novak and Tom Gribbins. The daughter of Slovakian immigrants who settled in Chicago, Irene was the third child in a family of ten, and even as a small child, she helped in the family bakery. When she reached age twenty, Irene left home to begin her Harvey Girl adventures. Her first job was at the large Harvey hotel Gran Quivira in Clovis, New Mexico. After a couple of years, Irene transferred to the Harvey House in Bakersfield, California, then went to work at La Posada in 1930. During these years, a Harvey Girl's usual pay was twenty-five

Harvey Girl Sue Wetzel began work at Havasu in Seligman, Arizona, in 1919 and later worked at La Posada in Winslow. *Courtesy of Arizona State Library, Archives and Public Records, History and Archives Division, Phoenix, No. 01-4791.*

dollars a month plus tips. Irene would routinely send her salary home to her family and lived off of her tips.

Tom Gribbins was born in Sacramento, California; however, after the death of his mother when he was a baby, he and his sister lived with aunts in Kansas and attended a Catholic boarding school in Oklahoma. Tom was working as a cook at La Posada when Irene came there as a Harvey Girl. The couple married in August 1930 with their Harvey friends in attendance. Frank Tyrell, another La Posada cook, was best man, and Marie Fuller, a Harvey Girl, was Irene's maid of honor. The couple's friends presented them with a camera and case as a wedding gift, and the photos of Tom and Irene included here were taken with that camera, which is now lovingly preserved by their granddaughter, Debbie Martin Cable, the daughter of the Gribbins' only child, Delores.

Irene Novak (*back of row*) with unidentified Harvey Girls in front of the original Harvey House in Winslow, Arizona, which, after La Posada was built, was converted into a dormitory for the waitresses. *Courtesy of Debbie Martin Cable.*

Above: Thomas Gribbin (*center*) with unidentified kitchen workers in the garden of La Posada. *Courtesy of Debbie Martin Cable.*

Left: Irene and Tom Gribbin after their marriage in 1930. Both were Harvey employees at La Posada in Winslow, Arizona. *Courtesy of Debbie Martin Cable.*

Tom worked at the "Century of Progress" Chicago World's Fair (1933–34) and was also able to find work for several of Irene's brothers there, which made him a hero to her family. Tom was also a cook in the navy and later worked for the railroad. In a recent telephone interview, the Gribbins's granddaughter said, "Both Tom and Irene worked and worked. My grandmother worked more than she took care of her daughter, who often lived with her grandparents. Irene and Tom divorced after fifteen years of marriage and Irene continued to work in the restaurant business. After La Posada closed, she continued to work as a waitress and also took jobs as a hostess and management including the historic Wigwam Resort near Phoenix. My grandmother worked well into her seventies and, as she had done with her family in the early days, she would send money home to her daughter and grandchildren. That's just who she was. She worked so she could take care of others."

A native of Saskatoon, Saskatchewan, Helene Hartney and her family came to Winslow to visit relatives on the advice of their doctor, who thought the desert climate would be good for their health. Helene and her younger sister, Margaret, soon got jobs as Harvey Girls working the lunch counters. The girls were allowed to live at home. "I had lived a very sheltered life, and Winslow was very open with bars, saloons and so forth," Helene said. "It was very different from what I knew and I was very shy. Everyone teased me about my Canadian accent and my Irish red hair. I loved everything about being a Harvey Girl. I met Robert Taylor, Alice Faye, Monty Woolley, Charles Lindbergh—all the famous people who came through on the Santa Fe."

Hoping to earn enough money to pay her nursing school tuition, Thalia Hosier went to work at La Posada after graduating from high school. She remembered the summer of 1934 as "a fun experience. We met a lot of different people and it was a good education about people." Thalia lived at home and earned twenty-five dollars a month plus one meal a day. One of her memories illustrates the sometimes hectic pace of serving Harvey House customers as well as a commitment to service. There was some water on the floor by the kitchen door from a leaking ice tub as Thalia stepped out into the dining room with plates of food for five of her customers. She slipped in the water and hit the floor, with plates and food flying everywhere. The manager, Omer Dooms, witnessed the catastrophe and calmly called out, "Thalia's on the floor. Duplicate her order." Thalia quickly changed to a clean uniform and returned to the kitchen in time to finish serving her customers. After leaving La Posada at the end of the summer as planned, Thalia attended nursing school in California and graduated in 1938. She worked in a children's hospital in Los Angeles and, after the war, returned to Winslow, where she worked in a private hospital. She later married Casey Gondek and was the secretary-treasurer of their family lumber and home repair business until her death in 1996. Through the years, Thalia credited her Harvey Girl training for her skill in working with the public.

In 1935, Ruby Gardner and a girlfriend made the sixty-mile trip from Snowflake, in southern Arizona, to Winslow to work as Harvey Girls at the La Posada. At a Harvey Girl reunion in 1992, Ruby described an early morning experience at the lunch counter:

"I went in at 4:00 a.m. and was making the fresh coffee," recalled Ruby Gardner McHood, "when a male customer asked me 'Do you make good coffee?' I replied, 'I don't know. I don't drink coffee, so I just make it the way they tell me.' He exclaimed, 'Everyone who works for Fred Harvey drinks coffee!' I could only say, 'I'm sorry. I just make it,' and kept working. Later, a friend told me that had been Fred Harvey himself, but I didn't get fired." This is a good example of misinformation perpetuated in Harvey Houses along the Santa Fe line from Texas to California. Fred Harvey died in 1901, thirty-six years before Ruby was serving coffee at La Posada.

The very early morning situation was unusual for Ruby, as she most often worked the counter on the 10:00 a.m. to 2:00 p.m. shift and occasionally served at one of the many banquets. "I was glad to work the middle shift. The early shift had to polish all that silverware every morning," she said. "Being a Harvey Girl meant you were special, because they hired you for your character. You were looked up to and respected." Ruby remembered that the pay wasn't much. "Just twenty-five dollars a month, but we got our meals, rooms, uniforms and kept all of our tips. We didn't spend much. We were young and didn't think we worked hard. Also, this was during the Depression, and jobs were hard to get. If you had one, you really appreciated it."

Within two years, Ruby had fallen in love with Hubert "Mac" McHood, and even though Fred Harvey was now allowing married women to work as Harvey Girls, Ruby resigned so she could be a full-time wife.

Virginia Schardein's cousin was a head waitress at the Bisonti Harvey Hotel in Hutchinson, Kansas, and in 1936, she recommended Virginia to join the staff as a Harvey Girl. In 1940, Virginia came to work at La Posada. She described the demands of the waitresses: "A Harvey Girl's work was never done. When they weren't serving customers, they were to fold

A group of Harvey Girls have some fun with World War II soldiers who came through Winslow, Arizona, on a troop train and stopped at La Posada for a meal. *Courtesy of Arizona State Library, Archives and Public Records, History and Archives Division, Phoenix, No. 01-4731.*

napkins, polish silver and clean and refill all of the condiment containers. No matter how busy we were, we were expected to give each new customer a menu and a glass of water." Virginia recalls seeing Clark Gable and Carole Lombard entering the dining room at La Posada just as she was getting off work. She may have just missed receiving a generous tip, as there are several Harvey Girl stories about Gable's reputation for leaving a silver dollar for his waitresses at a time when a dime was the normal tip. Virginia transferred to the Alvarado in Albuquerque, where she worked for a short while before returning to Winslow to marry Al Graff. "I made him chase me!" The couple married in 1947 and settled in Winslow.

Harvey Girl Jessie Philips recalled being a Harvey Girl during World War II. "The troop trains came through from early morning to late at night filled with young men going to the West Coast to be shipped out to fight the Japanese," Jessie remembered. "We worked hard to feed them, and the GIs were nice and appreciated everything." Jessie recalled one soldier who wanted her to sit with him and talk. "I didn't want to. You really didn't have the time. Anyway, a week or so later, I got this letter addressed to 'Harvey Girl No. 13, Winslow, Ariz.' We wore numbers on our uniforms, and the mailman knew just where to deliver the letter. In the letter, the soldier apologized and said he hadn't meant to embarrass me. He was just lonesome and wanted to talk to a girl. I was touched," Jessie said. "I sure wish I had kept his letter."

5

THE CANYON

When the railroad to the South Rim of the Grand Canyon was completed in 1901, tourism at the canyon quickly increased. Now, those wanting to experience the canyon could pay three dollars and ninety-five cents and reach the rim from Williams in three hours. Before, this excursion involved a twelve-hour "teeth-rattling" stagecoach ride that would set you back twenty dollars. By 1906, the Santa Fe was operating two daily trains to and from Williams to the Grand Canyon. Each train was usually filled to capacity.

El Tovar (est. 1905)

El Tovar (decorated by Mary Colter and designed by architect Charles Whittlesey) was built at a reported cost of $250,000 (the equivalent of $6,420,000 in 2019). The hotel opened four years after Fred Harvey's death; however, his oldest son, Ford, had been trained to continue the family business, and he, along with loyal managers and superintendents, saw the massive project of El Tovar successfully to its completion. Early reports of the El Tovar declared that "for novelty of architecture, design and convenience for the tourist public the new building will be unsurpassed." The landmark Harvey hotel was named for Pedro del Tovar, who was traditionally credited with being the first white man to penetrate the "mysterious depths" of the

Grand Canyon. The landmark structure, with one hundred guest rooms, would somehow achieve the essence of a timeworn Swiss tavern within an immense log house. The vast interior of El Tovar was designed with intimate alcoves such as private dining rooms, a mezzanine-level ladies' lounging room overlooking the lobby, an art room and a music room. Indoor recreation could be found in the billiards room, and the roof garden provided yet another view of the canyon. Colorful rugs and pottery added warmth and intimacy to seating areas in the large lobby decorated with imposing trophy heads, and outside guests could lounge on large, overreaching porches less than thirty feet from the South Rim.

Originally, room rates at El Tovar were four dollars per night for a single room, and with luck, you would have a spectacular sunrise view. Breakfast and lunch were one dollar, and a full-course dinner was one dollar and fifty cents. Of course, the costs of overnight accommodations have increased considerably through the years, and reservations should be secured well in advance of your visit; however, you'll be surrounded by the same dark beam ceilings, large fireplaces and tall windows overlooking the dramatic view of the Grand Canyon.

During the early 1900s, there were many newspaper accounts of Ford Harvey's travels to the Grand Canyon. These trips were usually business-related, and he often accompanied a writer from an eastern newspaper or national magazine; however, there were also hunting and leisure trips with contemporaries and family. Within a year after completion of El Tovar, Mrs.

El Tovar at the Grand Canyon in 1907 shortly after it opened. The reported cost of the Fred Harvey hotel was $250,000. *Courtesy of Tom Taylor.*

An intimate alcove in El Tovar known as the ladies' lounging room, where female guests could visit and enjoy refreshments. *Courtesy of Michael McMillan.*

The El Tovar lobby soon after the hotel was built. Little has changed, and today, visitors enjoy the same rustic ambiance. *Courtesy of Tom Taylor.*

The Start from El Tovar, Grand Canyon, Arizona.
COPYRIGHT 1907 BY FRED HARVEY

As early as 1907, guests at El Tovar were provided with tours in horse-drawn wagons. These excursions were a forerunner of the Indian Detours organized by Fred Harvey in the mid-1920s. *Courtesy of Tom Taylor.*

Ford (Judy) Harvey, along with her children, Kathleen and Fred Harvey, and their tutor traveled (by train, of course) to the canyon accompanied by two experienced Grand Canyon guides.

BRIGHT ANGEL LODGE (EST. 1935)

Fred Harvey's Bright Angel Lodge, designed by Mary Colter, was completed in 1935 and still provides accommodations with an atmosphere of vintage lodging. As early as 1896, J. Wilbur Thurber established a Bright Angel Camp that was merely a cabin used as an office and several tents that were rented to tourists. Later, the Bright Angel Camp evolved into a "neat arrangement of well-built cottages with sanitary rooms" that cost seventy-five cents per day, and meals in the adjacent thirty-eight-stool Harvey café annex began at thirty-five cents. The new Bright Angel Lodge had over seventy guest rooms with a mix of southwestern, mission and rustic furnishings and offered travelers all of the amenities and services expected from Fred Harvey. Bright Angel Lodge continues to be a popular

Fred Harvey's Bright Angel Lodge on the rim of the Grand Canyon. *Courtesy of Michael McMillan.*

resting place for visitors to the Grand Canyon. In addition to overnight accommodations, the lodge also features a gift shop, two restaurants, a lounge and an ice cream fountain.

PHANTOM RANCH (EST. 1920)

When the National Park Service considered building a permanent tourist facility on the floor of the Grand Canyon, it looked to the Fred Harvey company and designer Mary Colter. The site is on the north side of the Colorado River near where it joins Bright Angel Creek and Phantom Creek. Originally, the structures were to be named Roosevelt's Chalets in honor of President Theodore Roosevelt, whose enthusiasm for the Grand Canyon had helped bring it into the National Park System in 1919. However, Colter insisted that if her plan were to be used, then the name for a series of cabins utilizing on-site fieldstone and rough-hewn wood would be Phantom Ranch.

The project was completed in 1920, and in typical Fred Harvey fashion, the lodge was staffed with attractive, well-educated young women. During

Phantom Ranch on the floor of the Grand Canyon. This is perhaps Fred Harvey's most remote Harvey House. *Courtesy of Special Collections, University of Arizona Libraries, Fred Harvey collection (AZ 326).*

the three winter seasons from 1933 to 1936, the Civilian Conservation Corps Company 818, composed of forty-five men, made many improvements to the site and its accessible trails. The work was grueling, and everything except water had to be packed in by mule: wheelbarrows, shovels, picks, crowbars, drills and bits, gasoline and motor oil. One member of the company remarked, upon reaching the worksite at the bottom of the canyon, "I thought I had reached the end of the world!"

Currently, the site includes cabins, two dormitories each for men and women, a restaurant, a mule corral, emergency medical facilities and a ranger station. At 4,800 feet below the South Rim of the Grand Canyon, Phantom Ranch is certainly the least convenient Harvey facility; however, the experience of staying at the rustic lodge nestled into the glorious, natural surroundings makes it worth the trip.

There are other structures at the Grand Canyon designed by Mary Colter and managed by the Fred Harvey company.

The Hopi House was built east of El Tovar and opened the same year as the hotel. The structure was designed to resemble a Hopi dwelling and serves as a curio shop and sales outlet for Native American items. Hermit's Rest and the Lookout Studio opened in 1914 providing tourists with a rest stop and a spectacular view of the canyon. The Watchtower, completed in 1932, is a stone tower fashioned after an Indian kiva. This multilevel building features the art of Hopi artist Fred Kabotie and Fred Geary, an artist employed by the Fred Harvey company.

The El Tovar, Bright Angel Lodge and Phantom Ranch still prevail among the glorious setting of the Grand Canyon. Considering these shrines to Fred Harvey hospitality, it is easy for us to understand why every Harvey Girl's dream was to work here. Alice Steele, the employment manager for the Fred Harvey company for over thirty years, reported many requests from Harvey Girls to place them in the Grand Canyon for the summer.

A Harvey Girl at the Grand Canyon had to be an extremely efficient waitress to handle the volume of diners during peak tourist season. As stringent as the Harvey rules were across the system, requirements were even more rigorous for the young women who worked round-the-clock shifts at the Grand Canyon.

The young women lived in the girls' dormitory, which was named Colter Hall in honor of its designer, Mary Colter. Work shifts were often divided between the informal, family-friendly Bright Angel Lodge and the

Left: A typical wool Navajo rug similar to those sold in the Hopi House at the Grand Canyon. *Courtesy of Skip Gentry's Fred Harvey Memorabilia Collection.*

Right: A Fred Harvey tag on a rug guaranteeing it as an authentic Native American product. *Courtesy of Skip Gentry's Fred Harvey Memorabilia Collection.*

A sampling of authentic Fred Harvey bracelets. Jewelry such as this was sold in Harvey House curio shops throughout the Southwest. *Courtesy of Skip Gentry's Fred Harvey Memorabilia Collection.*

more formal, elegant El Tovar. The Grand Canyon was certainly the most beautiful site for Harvey's hotels, and nowhere else along the Santa Fe line did Harvey Girls work in the midst of hundreds of young men in the employ of Fred Harvey—cowboys, mechanics, trail guides (later called wranglers) and mule skinners. Often, these men would put together a band and gather in the lounge at Bright Angel Lodge to play at a dance for tourists and employees alike. Young women also had a variety of opportunities to work for the Harvey system at the canyon other than as waitresses—in the curio shops, as a clerk in the hotel or arranging detour trips. Former Harvey Girl Betty Meyer explained, "Life at the Canyon centered on the storied El Tovar hotel and the daily Santa Fe trains. It seemed that anyone who lived there was a Harvey person, one way or another."

Edwin "Ed" Wayne Cummings went to the Grand Canyon in 1919 to work as a forest ranger. Ed had studied geology and decided a job with Fred Harvey as a trail guide would be interesting. A family history describes his daily trips on inner canyon trails, guiding parties to the river, as affording him endless opportunities to increase his knowledge of geology through study of formations along the trail. "He was never happier than when conducting geological groups into the canyon, or guiding some eminent scientist on pack trips off the beaten path."

In 1921, Ed married Ida Goodman, who, after graduating from high school and business college, began working for Fred Harvey in Kansas City. She took advantage of the opportunity to transfer from one Harvey House to another along the Santa Fe railroad line, moving to Albuquerque, Belen and Gallup, New Mexico, and Winslow, Ash Fork and Williams, Arizona, before landing a coveted spot at the Grand Canyon.

In the mid-1930s, Ed worked with Fred Harvey architect and designer Mary Colter on the fireplace in what is now the history room of the Bright Angel Lodge. Ed's son recounted his father's description of the process: "They made the fireplace using stones taken from the walls of the canyon. Water-worn schist from the Colorado River level formed the hearth of the fireplace. Each succeeding layer of the canyon wall is duplicated in the layers of stone that form the fireplace. Kaibab limestone, the surface layer of the canyon, forms the top of the ten-foot high chimney." Ed Cummings passed away in 1951, and Ida continued to live at the canyon until her death in 1980, having spent over fifty years there. Both of them are buried in the Grand Canyon Cemetery.

Kathryn Massey, who was born in Kansas and later lived with family in Arkansas, was hired as a Harvey Girl in 1924 after stating her age as eighteen rather than her true age of sixteen. She wanted the job and knew that it was illegal for a minor to travel out of state unaccompanied to work. Kathryn's ultimate goal was to work at the El Tovar at the Grand Canyon, and that required a minimum of five years' experience as a Harvey Girl. She arrived in Williams, Arizona, planning to work at Fray Marcos to meet that requirement. However, after six months, true love trumped the canyon—Kathryn married Don Massey, and her Harvey days were over. Many years later, Kathryn did work at the Grand Canyon, but not for Fred Harvey. Instead, she was employed at the Red Feather Lodge in the Grand Canyon Village.

For all the romantic notions of the femininity and grace of Harvey Girls, a certain amount of toughness was required. The job was physically demanding, and the work hours were long. It took a specific type of young woman to meet the challenges. One such Harvey Girl was Lorraine Ida McKinley Clark, who worked at the Grand Canyon in the 1920s. Lorraine didn't share much about her life with family, and it wasn't until after she died that her granddaughter Kelly Clark Ludlum learned that her grandmother had been a Harvey Girl. Exactly how Lorraine made her way from Kingfisher, Oklahoma, to the Grand Canyon isn't known; however, it is possible she rode the Santa Fe straight west from her hometown and, almost one thousand miles later, began her Harvey Girl career at the canyon. Lorraine is remembered as "very outdoorsy," and her granddaughter remembers being required to "set a table" during a camping trip. The former Harvey Girl got out a ruler to measure that the place setting was the required distance from the edge. Well after her ninetieth birthday, Lorraine was doing pushups and mowing her lawn.

Bertha Parker grew up in Arkansas, and after completing a few semesters at the University of Arkansas, the young woman's only goal in life was to leave rural Arkansas and go to California. "There wasn't any work at home; there wasn't much work anywhere. My ambition was to somehow get to California. Everyone thought California was the place to go in the early 1920s." Bertha's father didn't think much of folks who worked along the railroad and didn't think working as a waitress at a Harvey House was a proper job for his daughter. Against his demands, she sent a photo and application to the Fred Harvey offices in Kansas City. "My mother saw there was nothing else for me to do. Besides, when I was sent a railroad pass to Las Vegas, New Mexico, to work as a Harvey Girl at the Castaneda, I knew it was a lot closer to California than Arkansas, and I wouldn't be stopped."

After six months in Las Vegas, Bertha had earned a free train pass and vacation time with her family in Arkansas. During her time off, she received word that there was an immediate need for Harvey Girls to work over the summer at the Grand Canyon. "Arizona was even closer to California, so off I went!"

Bertha worked in the dining room and at the lunch counter at Bright Angel Lodge. She lived in the dormitory across the road from the hotel. She recalled in an interview that in 1926, she was paid forty dollars a month plus room and board. "I saved some money—the tips were very good at the canyon." Bertha's experience confirms the notion that most Harvey Girls thought of the Grand Canyon as the best work assignment a Harvey Girl could have. Not only would you work in one of the most beautiful natural settings in the country, but working at the canyon provided the heady opportunity of serving travelers from all over the United States and foreign countries. As Bertha remembered, tips were good, and a Harvey Girl looking for a husband had so many "Harvey Guys" to choose from.

At the canyon, Bertha met Charles Maddux, who worked for Fred Harvey driving the canyon touring cars. "I quit my job after six months," Bertha said. "I was in love! Charles and I left the canyon in his Chevrolet touring car, drove to Flagstaff and were married." Charles continued to drive a touring car, and Bertha worked as a Harvey Girl when extra help was needed. Fred Harvey provided tent houses for married employees. "One room with a pot-bellied stove, canvas walls, a wood floor. We got by." After two years, the couple moved to Kingman, Arizona, where Charles established a trucking company.

A Fred Harvey postcard featuring the coffee shop at Bright Angel Lodge at the Grand Canyon. *Courtesy of Michael McMillan.*

The early 1930s found twenty-three-year-old Thelma Drzewiecki a widow with an infant daughter. That was the year Thelma says she became a lady. The daughter of homesteaders from Nara Visa, a tiny community in eastern New Mexico, had many jobs throughout her adult life—ranch girl, World War II WAC, sales and advertising agent, gold prospector—but the one that stands out above all others was Harvey Girl line waitress. That experience is what, Thelma believes, transformed her into a lady. Her husband died in a construction accident, leaving Thelma with an eighteen-month-old daughter to care for. Thelma had taken a job in a locally owned café in Albuquerque, but her wages and tips fell short of meeting her financial obligations. A friend suggested that she apply at the Alvarado Harvey hotel, where they were hiring line waitresses and guaranteeing sixty dollars per month plus room and board. "I had no idea what a line waitress was, but the money sounded good." Thelma soon learned that you would be "living out of a suitcase from one end of the Santa Fe Railroad to the other; from Chicago to Los Angeles. I was told that when I was done with this job, I would be able to serve anywhere in the world." The training was difficult, and the new Harvey Girls were under complete control of a matron who was responsible for their work and living arrangements. "She had full control of us…ladies. I mean, we were turned from little street girls to ladies immediately."

An impressive thunderbird icon sits above the large stone fireplace in the lobby of Bright Angel Lodge. *Courtesy of Tom Taylor.*

When her training was complete, Thelma was sent to Gallup, New Mexico, and then to the Grand Canyon. "Believe me, it wasn't all Irish linens and white uniforms! I remember a fistfight at the canyon between a group of 'Chicago girls' and the 'Western girls.' Of course, we were all Harvey Girls and models of propriety and politeness when we were working." Thelma remembers that the only recreation at the time was to ride an old bus down to Flagstaff. "These kids today think this pot [marijuana] is great. I remember smoking fresh grown pot from the northern rim of the canyon, where it grows wild. So we'd ride the bus to Flagstaff and get high on pot. Once, we went into a restaurant and were so loud the manager asked us to leave. This was definitely unapproved recreation for a Harvey Girl!"

Dorothy Bailey Hunt was in Arizona for a monthlong vacation in 1935 when a friend of her parents asked Dorothy to work in her store in Navajo on Route 66. Although Dorothy was often interviewed about her experiences as a Harvey Girl, I couldn't find out what about this "temporary" job prompted her to stay in Arizona rather than return to her home in California. However, after two years in Navajo, Dorothy moved to Winslow and worked at local cafés, then moved to some popular Winslow bars to work as a bartender. In 1942, Dorothy met railroader Richard Hunt, and two years later, they were married and Richard was hired as a brakeman on the Williams–to–Grand Canyon line, so they moved to the canyon.

Dorothy's experience made her a prime candidate to work for the Fred Harvey restaurants in the bustling Grand Canyon. She worked at the Bright Angel Lodge and El Tovar and wore an all-white Harvey Girl uniform when she worked special parties after 8:00 p.m. for organizations such as the Shriners and the Elks. In a newspaper interview, Dorothy remembered the "beautiful ice carvings made by the French chef Marcel Fordeau for the parties to go with the elaborately prepared buffet meals complete with a whole roasted pig or a forty-pound ham served." Dorothy worked at a time when Harvey Girls didn't always wear the iconic black-and-white uniform. "I wore an Indian squaw dress and Navajo jewelry and earned $128 plus tips every two weeks when I worked as a cocktail waitress and then bartender at the canyon."

Richard's Santa Fe job moved him to Winslow, and Dorothy became the bartender at the Bull Ring Bar at La Posada. During the next few years, as Richard got "bumped" between Santa Fe runs, the couple often moved between the canyon and Winslow. "When we returned to the canyon, I bartended at the Bright Angel. This was during the war, and there weren't

El Tovar Harvey Girls Dorothy Bailey Hunt (*center*) and Betty McCoy (*right*) are pictured in 1950. An unidentified Harvey Girl is on the left. *Courtesy of Arizona State Library, Archives and Public Records, History and Archives Division, Phoenix, No. 01-4746.*

Elaborate banquet serving table with ice sculpture for a special event at El Tovar in the 1970s. *Courtesy of Bill Orr.*

many men to fill these jobs." Dorothy has many good memories of working with other Harvey employees, but her memories of the canyon are most precious. "We would sit along the rim in front of Bright Angel at night and watch the moon, the clouds—everything over the canyon. I loved it!" Dorothy recalled the meaningful sunrise service held at Easter each year. "Senator Barry Goldwater often attended." The Hunts even spent a few winters at the Grand Canyon. "One year, we had about three feet of snow. It was beautiful!" In 1958, Richard and Dorothy permanently moved to Winslow, and Dorothy became a stay-at-home mom for their two children.

Betty Priest began her tenure at the Grand Canyon in July 1926 after answering a call for applicants issued by the Fred Harvey company in Kansas City, Missouri, a year earlier. A girlfriend issued a dare for Betty to apply, which she did. Betty was promptly hired and sent to Hutchinson, Kansas, for training. After working six months at the Alvarado in Albuquerque, New Mexico, she was sent to the canyon for the peak tourist season. Even though Betty was "put off" by the strict rules, she signed a six-month contract agreeing not to marry during that time. "We didn't get paid at first, but we got room and board while being trained." Trainees were introduced to gourmet foods and learned meat carving and proper ways of setting tables with fine linens and highly polished silverware. "Our training was precise and intense. It instilled sophistication and professionalism in a group of girls who mostly had no experience."

"At the canyon, we made our own entertainment. There was one building for recreation, so the fellows made up an orchestra of sorts, and we had dances. Not all Harvey employees were single; there were families, also. Children slept on pallets in the cloak hall while the adults danced away the evening. On Saturday night, there were movies; we had Sunday school, and sometimes there would be a minister who conducted a church service."

Within days of arriving at the canyon, Betty was noticed—and admired—from a distance by Bill Kent, a machinist who ran the icehouse. Bill told his friends that he was going to marry the pretty, young Harvey Girl. Betty let it be known that he "didn't have a chance," because she had someone else in her life. Whoever the "someone" was must have been surprised when, within a month or so, Betty was wearing Kent's engagement ring. They married in October 1927 and enjoyed forty-seven and a half years together. Early in their married years, Betty went to Kansas City to help at the Harvey restaurant in Union Station during the 1928 Republican National Convention. "At the time, Harvey Girl tips averaged ten to twenty-five cents. I was overwhelmed with the sixty-seven dollars I received one night. Some men were playing poker, and I urged them to quit because their T-bone steaks were ready. One of them said the waitress could have the pot and swept a pile of silver dollars toward me. Can you imagine? It was a fortune!" Through the years after her Harvey days, Betty said she tried working in a regular restaurant. "I was appalled at the way they sling things around. There is nothing like a Harvey Girl."

While many young women were drawn by the adventure and somewhat daring life of a Harvey Girl at the Grand Canyon, for some, the job was an answer to a desperate situation, particularly during the Depression years. Lucille Oswald grew up on a small Ozark farm in Missouri, the family was poor and she remembers that there was never enough food. Lucille remembers that her sisters "packed me off to Fred Harvey." She first worked in Ash Fork, Arizona, and then at El Tovar and Bright Angel Lodge at the Grand Canyon for three years. "They fed me. I tried my best. I wasn't about to go back where there was no food." Among Lucille's best memories were "the men from the Peavine (a twisting rail line linking Prescott with Ash Fork) out of Prescott. They were very flirty, and I was shy. They managed to embarrass me."

6

ALWAYS GOOD EATS

*I*n the late nineteenth century, visionary Fred Harvey promised the Santa Fe Railroad top brass that he could establish restaurants along the railroad line that would have the best reputation for delicious food served in pleasant surroundings. Harvey believed that folks would ride the train just to eat in his Harvey Houses. His vision became a reality as thousands of train passengers enjoyed first-class dining opportunities throughout the Southwest.

HOLBROOK (1884–1886)

The railroad arrived in Holbrook in 1881, and three years later, Fred Harvey moved five old boxcars onto a rail siding there. The outside of the train cars had a fresh coat of red paint, and they were embellished with Native American symbols; however, they didn't appear to have the attributes that folks had come to expect from a Harvey House. Certainly, train passengers were pleasantly surprised upon entering the "dining room" boxcar, where tables were set with linen, silver, crystal and fresh flowers from California.

The Holbrook location was open from 1884 to 1886, and I believe it is likely that some sections of this makeshift Harvey House were not so elegantly decorated and appealed to the railroad workmen, cowboys and other locals who needed a place to get a decent meal.

There was virtually no law in Holbrook well into the twentieth century. Violence ranged from Apache and Navajo raids on settlers to violent disputes between sheep ranchers and cattle ranchers. In 1886, the population of Holbrook was about 250, and 26 people died violent deaths, making a citizen's odds of being murdered that year something over one in ten.

I couldn't find any history of Harvey Girls who worked in Holbrook, which leads me to believe that the Harvey "guys" from the kitchen may have also been the waitstaff. After all, it was said that the town was "no place for women and children."

What we do know is that Holbrook is an example of how Fred Harvey could maintain his standards of service and quality of food even when faced with a less-than-ideal setting. We also know that Holbrook successfully overcame its early Wild West days and developed into a community with a current population of over five thousand in the midst of the natural beauty of the Painted Desert, the Petrified Forest National Park and the nearby Canyon de Chelly.

KINGMAN (1901–1938)

Kingman was the site of the westernmost Arizona Harvey House and provided Fred Harvey hospitality at a lunchroom, dining room and newsstand. The town was named for Lewis Kingman, a railroad surveyor who supervised the building of the railroad from Winslow to Kingman.

The Kingman Harvey House operated trackside until 1938. During those thirty-seven years, it was the social hub of the town, with many civic groups meeting there for lunch. The dining room also hosted many bridal showers and women's teas. The building was renovated for use by soldiers training at the Kingman Airfield in 1942 and was later used by the American Legion. A fire in the summer of 1952 destroyed the interior, leaving the building an empty shell. It was demolished a year later, leaving nothing but the concrete platform where it once stood.

Bernice Black grew up in Nebraska, and in 1926, when she was nineteen, she went to visit a cousin in Topeka, Kansas. While she was there, she heard about the opportunities for young women to work for the Fred Harvey company. "My mother and family didn't think too much about my becoming a waitress, but I wanted to work." Bernice received her Harvey Girl training at the El Navajo Harvey House in Gallup, New Mexico, and signed a six-

The Harvey House trackside in Kingman, Arizona. *Courtesy of Special Collections, University of Arizona Libraries, Fred Harvey collection (AZ 326).*

The Kingman Harvey House lunch counter set in typical Fred Harvey style. *Courtesy of Special Collections, University of Arizona Libraries, Fred Harvey collection (AZ 326).*

The Harvey Girl staff at the Kingman Harvey House in the 1930s. *Courtesy of Arizona State Library, Archives and Public Records, History and Archives Division, Phoenix, No. 01-4748.*

month contract to work in Kingman, Arizona. She fondly remembered the camaraderie among Harvey employees. "We could not date Harvey employees, but we could date railroad men. The men who worked for the railroad had a real respect for the Harvey Girls. They treated us well, and there were many marriages." The desert of Arizona was shocking to Bernice, and after she had fulfilled her six-month contract, she was ready to go home and stay home. "After three weeks, I missed the desert so much I wrote the Kingman manager and asked if I could return. They said 'yes,' and I returned and stayed there a long, long time." Bernice worked as a Harvey Girl in Kingman, the Grand Canyon and at La Posada. When she was thirty-two, she married a railroad man. "That was pretty old to be getting married in those days!"

When Rose Tehan reported for her first job as a Harvey Girl in August 1929, the manager took one look at her and said, "Well, I suppose you don't know the difference between a plate and a platter." That was almost too much for the young woman who had left her home on a farm near Milwaukee, Wisconsin; endured an interview at the Fred Harvey offices in Chicago; and traveled almost 1,800 miles by train in the summer heat to reach Kingman, Arizona. By the end of her first day, Rose compared the pain in her legs and feet to the worst toothache ever, because she was not accustomed to walking on concrete and tile floors. "There was so much I didn't know, and I was so far from home," she said. "One of my first customers left a dime tip under his plate at the lunch counter. I was so deeply humiliated and embarrassed by having been given what I considered alms that I cried. Of course, I soon learned that a dime tip in this far-flung part of the country was a good thing. And in spite of the bad start, I liked the job and liked being deep in the heart of the West!"

Rose lived with the other Harvey Girls on the second floor of the Harvey House about thirty feet from the main line of the Santa Fe. "We were usually so tired the trains didn't wake us." The manager who met Rose with the stern statement was very strict about keeping the Fred Harvey rules. This was an

Frankie Matthews, a busboy at the Kingman Harvey House, in 1928. *Courtesy of Old Trails Museum and Winslow Historical Society.*

unusual attitude for a Harvey House manager, as most were somewhat lenient with the rules as long as the young women were efficient and dependable. "We were forbidden to date other Harvey employees, and those who broke the rules would find themselves with a one-way pass home. Curfew time, including nights when there were dances, was 11:00 p.m., and violations of curfew would also result in a pass home for the offender."

In the late 1920s, the Kingman restaurant fed two or three passenger trains a day, with approximately three hundred passengers aboard each, most of whom usually ate at the Harvey House. "Feeding that many hungry people in thirty minutes was a big job, but it was also fun," Rose said. "When the time was about up, the engineer would give a warning toot, and the conductor would come through the lunch counter and dining room making sure that nobody was left before he signaled for the train to start moving." She recalls when a group of Swedish Olympic contestants stopped in Kingman to eat: "They were really huge, blond men who ate a tremendous amount of food." After seven months in Kingman, Rose used her free pass and took the train to San Francisco for a "sightseeing vacation." When she returned, she asked for a transfer to Ash Fork, and after a short time there, moved on to Fray Marcos

Mary Eads (*left*) and Ora Lee Cooper (*right*), Kingman Harvey Girls, in 1928. *Courtesy of Old Trails Museum and Winslow Historical Society.*

in Williams, where she remained until 1933. "My pay increased from my starting pay of thirty-five dollars a month to eventually fifty dollars. However, when the Depression hit, Fred Harvey, along with most other employers, had to cut back, and we were asked to take a voluntary cut to forty-five dollars." Rose managed to save enough money to go to Phoenix, where she enrolled in business college and took typing and office procedures with the idea of preparing for a better job. While in Phoenix, she met and married Clarence Stacy, an agent for New York Life Insurance Company, and they moved to Flagstaff. Rose coupled her Harvey Girl customer service skills with the business skills she learned in business college and held many responsible office jobs through the years. Eventually, she was elected treasurer of Coconino County, where she served for almost thirty years until her retirement in 1981.

PAINTED DESERT INN (EST. 1947)

In 1947, the Fred Harvey company bought the Painted Desert Inn, a pueblo-style structure near the front gate of the northern third of the Petrified Forest. This Harvey House catered to automobile traffic along a lonely stretch of Route 66. Originally built by Herbert David Lore of Holbrook in 1924 of petrified wood held together with mud mortar, the inn was originally called Stone Tree House.

The building was sold to the National Park Service in 1936 with a relatively simple plan to rehabilitate the inn and provide running water and electricity. Closer inspection revealed that the building was structurally unsound and restoration would not be feasible. New construction was the only choice; however, these were the Depression years, and the National Park Service could not undertake the building of a new inn. A "workaround" plan was devised. Rebuilding materials were recategorized as "thinning materials" considered necessary for forest maintenance. The materials arrived, the Civilian Conservation Corps provided the labor and the Painted Desert Inn was reconstructed. The total cost of the project was $20,000. The walls were covered with lime plaster and putty, and the ceilings were constructed of pine beams for a traditional pueblo look. The floors were concrete, flagstone and wood. The CCC crews also cut, shaped and hand-punched tin light fixtures and stunning hand-painted skylight panels. These have been preserved and are still part of the interior design of the building.

Above: Present-day photo of the Painted Desert Inn. Built in 1924, it was purchased by the Fred Harvey company in 1947. *Courtesy of Kathy Weir.*

Left: Rachel Ramirez was a Harvey Girl at the Painted Desert Inn in the late 1940s. *Courtesy of the Ramirez family.*

The Painted Desert Inn reopened in 1940, closed in 1942 during World War II and opened again in 1947, with Harvey Girls providing travelers a choice of cold or hot sandwiches, salads and refreshing items from the soda fountain accompanied by the well-regarded Fred Harvey service. Mary Colter was called into action to create a striking interior. She chose a new interior color scheme and added strategically placed plate-glass windows to take advantage of the magnificent view. Colter's site-sensitive touch produced

One of the murals at the Painted Desert Inn painted by Hopi artist Frank Kabotie. *Courtesy of Library of Congress, Prints & Photographs Division.*

a mixture of Spanish and Indian pueblo styles and featured beautiful murals in the dining room and lunchroom painted by Hopi artist Fred Kabotie.

There is an oft-told story about a visit by Albert Einstein to the Painted Desert Inn and his exploration through the surrounding landscape accompanied by a Harvey Girl. During the walk, the young woman pointed out a sign referring to some petrified logs that read: "Six Million Years Old." Einstein thought for a few seconds and remarked, "I believe it is not six million, but sixty million."

Raymond Roberts and his wife, Stella, worked for Fred Harvey in Needles, California, and at La Posada in Winslow, Arizona, before moving to the Painted Desert Inn. Raymond was a chef, and at the inn, Stella assisted him in the kitchen. During the summer beginning in 1947, Stella's nieces Nora and Rachel Ramirez were Harvey Girls serving tourists who veered off of Highway 66 to enjoy Fred Harvey hospitality.

Nora had worked as a bus girl at La Posada in Winslow the summer before her freshman year of high school. The next year, she, with her sister, began spending the summer months working at the Fred Harvey Painted Desert Inn, an hour and a half from Winslow.

"Rachel, who is two years younger, and I worked with three other waitresses. Our brother, Mac, was the busboy," Nora said in a recent interview. "Our day began around 7:00 or 8:00 in the morning and ended at 6:00 in the evening. This was my summer job while I attended Winslow High School. We were provided room and board. The only reason our mother allowed us to live and work away from home was because our aunt was also working there." Other employees at the time were a hostess and a clerk in the gift shop.

Left: Harvey Girl Nora Ramirez atop the Painted Desert Inn sign. *Courtesy of the Ramirez family.*

Below: The lunchroom of the Painted Desert Inn is open to visitors, although there is no longer food service. *Courtesy of Sara Belknap.*

The Harvey standards were maintained in this small Harvey House. "The hostess would check us to be sure we were dressed properly. We were required to wear stockings, a white uniform with a bow tie and we always had to wear a hairnet. When taking an order, we were taught to stand at the head of the table and, if we were serving a family, we took the food order from the man." Nora has fond memories of visiting with the tourists who came to the Painted Desert Inn. "People would come from all over. They usually had time to talk and seemed to enjoy telling us about where they lived and why they were visiting Arizona."

After graduating from high school, Nora worked for Fred Harvey at El Navajo in Gallup, New Mexico. "After a few months, I got homesick and went back to Winslow," Nora said. "Then, I decided I wanted to broaden my experiences and I joined the Air Force. I trained in San Antonio, Texas, and worked as a teletype operator in Washington, D.C., for a year before transferring to Germany." Nora met her husband, Michael Breeze, while in Germany, and the couple eventually settled in Winslow to raise their family that would total nine children—five boys and four girls. Michael worked for the Santa Fe railroad until his retirement, and the couple continues to live in Winslow.

The Painted Desert Inn closed in 1963, and after barely escaping demolition, it was reopened in 1976 as the Petrified Forest National Park Bicentennial Travel Center. In 1987, it was declared a National Historic Landmark. After months of reconstruction, it was reopened as a museum and souvenir store in May 2006. The inn now appears somewhat as it would have in 1949, with the Kabotie murals even more prominent in the sparse surroundings. Although there is no longer food service or overnight accommodations, the building is open to visitors year-round.

7

HARVEY CIGARS, POSTCARDS AND CANDY

*C*ertainly, the original Harvey newsstand at the Phoenix train depot was much smaller than the prominent newsstand inside the large Mission Revival–style Union Station built in 1923. The new, prominent Fred Harvey newsstand beckoned train passengers with large open windows displaying the latest newspapers, magazines and books. Once you entered the newsstand, the array of merchandise could be irresistible.

In a sense, Fred Harvey newsstands were the twentieth-century forerunner of modern-day convenience stores. In many Harvey House locations, the newsstand was located inside the lunchroom; however, in larger train stations such as the one in Phoenix, it was usually a separate shop that opened into public space or directly onto the platform beside the train tracks. The amount and variety of merchandise offered was in proportion to the number of passengers that passed through the train station. The newsstand was usually staffed by male Harvey employees who were always impeccably dressed in dark suits and white shirts. A job as a cashier in a newsstand, especially one as large as the one in Phoenix, was often the first step toward being promoted to manager of a Harvey House.

Cigarettes and cigars were the prominent merchandise in every Fred Harvey newsstand. Large Lucky Strike posters featuring young beauties in shorts and ballet slippers declared, "It's toasted!" and "Lucky's are always kind to your throat!" Colorful advertising touted such products as "flat fifties"—thin, square tin boxes containing fifty cigarettes that were popular in the 1940s. The American Tobacco Company included this message

The Union Station in Phoenix, Arizona, didn't have a Harvey House; instead, there was a large, thriving Fred Harvey newsstand. *Courtesy of Michael McMillan.*

The Fred Harvey newsstand had three large display windows facing the high-traffic corridor of the Union Station in Phoenix. *Courtesy of Special Collections, University of Arizona Libraries, Fred Harvey collection (AZ 326).*

Souvenir spoons depicting scenes from the Grand Canyon were popular items sold in Harvey newsstands in Arizona. *Courtesy of Skip Gentry's Fred Harvey Memorabilia Collection.*

inside the tins: "These LUCKY STRIKE CIGARETTES will commend themselves to your critical approval. The additional 'toasting process' adds to the character and improves the taste of the fine tobacco." The Fred Harvey private brand of cigars, as well as Roi-Tan, Cremo and Prodigo, were sold with the promise: "We give discount on cigars bought by the box."

Chewing gum and candy were also big sellers. The Fred Harvey employees' newsletter, *Hospitality*, reported that "nearly 50,000 boxes of Harvey Girl chocolates sold although fresh fruit was often displayed on the counter as well." Newsstands were always framed with wire displays of postcards. The postcard business flourished after 1904, when Ford Harvey began working with the Detroit Publishing Company, which had developed a process for colorizing black-and-white photos. A good number of the postcards from the early Harvey days have survived and are often available for sale online. Many of the images in this book were digitized from original Harvey postcards from the collections of Michael McMillan and Tom Taylor, Harvey House historians.

Souvenirs were attractively displayed to appeal to train passengers. Miniature ceramic models of Harvey Girls sold for one dollar each and were some of the best-selling souvenirs. Keychains and letter openers, as well

The stereoscope was first introduced in 1939. Soon after, the Fred Harvey company produced these stereoscopes with scenes of the Grand Canyon and sold them in newsstands in Arizona. *Courtesy of Skip Gentry's Fred Harvey Memorabilia Collection.*

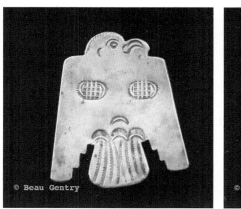 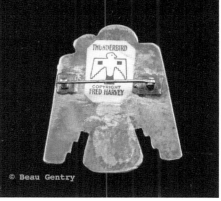

Left: The Fred Harvey company designed jewelry specifically for the tourist trade and often hired Native American silversmiths to make items to sell in Harvey newsstands and curio shops. *Courtesy of Skip Gentry's Fred Harvey Memorabilia Collection.*

Right: This particular thunderbird was authenticated as a Fred Harvey design and used on many jewelry pieces. *Courtesy of Skip Gentry's Fred Harvey Memorabilia Collection.*

As in many Harvey hotels, the newsstand was integrated into the lobby of the Havasu in Seligman, Arizona. *Courtesy of Special Collections, University of Arizona Libraries, Fred Harvey collection (AZ 326).*

as figurines and toy trucks, all clamored for the travelers' attention. Small items displayed on glass shelves were advertised as souvenirs that could be used for bridge card party prizes. The variety of merchandise was endless: cloisonné compacts, sewing notions, watches and brightly colored triangular felt pennants emblazoned with the state's name.

Solutions for the wide-ranging needs of a traveler were for sale at larger Harvey newsstands. These were listed alphabetically on multisided signs with the invitation to ask for articles not listed. Some of these items relieved a traveler's ills: Bromo Quinine cold tablets, Bromo Seltzer for the tummy, liniments, Listerine, Mentholatum and Lavoris. Men's garters and collar buttons were available, as well as cold cream, face powder, Kotex, nail files and perfume for the ladies. Perhaps the most useful remedy available at the newsstands was Cascaret. The advertising for these brown octagonal tablets—reputed to have a taste almost as pleasant as chocolate—promised to eliminate "Heartburn, Colic, Coated Tongue, Suspected Breath, Acid-rising-in-throat, Gas-belching, or an incipient Cold."

Fred Harvey newsstands were a very successful business, and throughout the Harvey system, many survived long after lunchrooms and dining rooms had closed. Fred Harvey business records indicate that by 1950, the company still maintained over one hundred newsstands.

8

HARVEY FARMS

PEACH SPRINGS (1884–1889) / DEL RIO (1912–1956)

Fresh food was always a priority for Fred Harvey, and the Harvey system of restaurants and hotels demanded a large, dependable supply. A Harvey House chef could purchase from local farmers if they met the Harvey standards for quality. However, in certain circumstances, the company could better control quality and food costs by establishing large, company-owned farms and ranches to supply their restaurants all along the Santa Fe line.

In Arizona, the original dairy farm was established in Peach Springs in the far northwest corner of Arizona. In 1884, a primitive Harvey House was established trackside in the small town for tourists who would, at that time, trek twenty miles north via Diamond Creek to the Grand Canyon. Peach Springs enjoyed some prosperity until a rail link was built from Williams to the South Rim of the Grand Canyon, and this Harvey House closed.

The first dairy in Arizona was moved from Peach Springs to Del Rio, in the northern reaches of Chino Valley, in 1912. Grace Converse lived with her husband, George Converse, for thirty years on the Del Rio ranch, located about twenty miles north of Prescott, working for Fred Harvey. "That place is home to me and the rest of the family; my kids were all raised there." The family lived in an ancient, thick-walled adobe with huge log beams and a two-foot-thick earthen roof that was originally meant to provide protection from Indian torches.

An original photograph showing an overview of the Fred Harvey farm in Del Rio, Arizona. *Courtesy of the George Converse family.*

"They had a big dairy herd and about two thousand laying hens," Grace said in an interview in the *Prescott Courier*. "It supplied all the milk and eggs to the western division of the famous Fred Harvey operation that fed travelers from San Bernardino [California] to Albuquerque [New Mexico]." George and Grace first came to Del Rio in 1927, and George was the farm manager for a few years before the dairy operation was closed. "We began to just grow silage for the stock that belonged to Harvey, like the dude mules," Grace said. "The Harvey people found out they could buy the milk and egg products they needed from sources closer to the various restaurants cheaper than they could raise it and ship it from the Arizona ranch."

The Del Rio ranch was a pasture for Hereford and Charolais cattle. It was the wintering ground for the famous mules that took tourists from the rim of the Grand Canyon down the Bright Angel Trail to the Phantom Ranch. "That was the finest string of mules you ever saw, and George spent a lot of time getting them ready for the trail each season," Grace said. "They were beautiful when they left here."

Of course, there were no Harvey Girls on the Del Rio ranch, and Grace did all of the cooking. "I was the cook, and I fed the crews, like when we had twenty-five to thirty men working for us from 1927 to 1933," she explained. "We were putting up silage and always had a lot of people around. During the Depression, there were always transients coming through, sometimes five or six a day, some with their families."

Approximately 200 acres of the farm remained under cultivation until 1945, when the operation was expanded to 550 acres after an artesian well was discovered. "Across the road, George discovered and opened up an artesian well that flowed at better than two thousand gallons a minute. Then

Egg cartons used at the Fred Harvey Ranch in Del Rio, Arizona. At one time, the ranch had a large dairy herd and over two thousand laying hens. *Courtesy of Skip Gentry's Fred Harvey Memorabilia Collection.*

we really raised hay!" Of the seven to eight hundred tons of hay produced by the ranch each year, half of it would go to the Grand Canyon to feed the mules and working stock there.

During the war, the farm raised turkeys. Grace remembered there being over five thousand per year to ship by train to Harvey Houses. "There was meat rationing on, and beef was hard to come by, so we raised turkeys for the company.

"When we first came to the farm, I couldn't figure out why anybody would want to live here," Grace said. "I thought it was a Godforsaken country. I wouldn't even let the kids out the back door by themselves, afraid they would get carried off by some animal. After a while, I got to love the place."

The Harvey organization sold the ranch in 1956, and the Converse family went to the Grand Canyon to work until George retired in 1965.

Water from nearby Del Rio Springs in Chino Valley was crucial to Fred Harvey and the Santa Fe. In 1901, the *Journal Miner* newspaper reported the capacity of the spring at "about 2,000,000 gallons a day and the daily pumping capacity about 500,000 gallons under 750 pounds of pressure." The system was put into operation in September 1901, and by mid-May 1902, the city council of Prescott voted to furnish water from Del Rio Springs to the Santa Fe for seventy-two cents per 6,600-gallon

George Converse (*pictured*) and his wife, Grace, managed the Fred Harvey Ranch in Del Rio, Arizona, from 1927 to 1957. *Courtesy of the George Converse family.*

tank carload. The railroad transported the potable water from Del Rio to the many locations along its northern Arizona lines, including the towns of Seligman, Ash Fork, Williams, Winslow and, eventually, the Grand Canyon (one hundred miles away). With a reliable water source, Ford Harvey and the Santa Fe now had everything in place to begin developing the Harvey properties at the Grand Canyon into a popular tourist destination.

9

FROM THE KITCHEN:
HARVEY HOUSE RECIPES

These Harvey House recipes and kitchen tips were featured in the *Santa Fe Employes' [sic] Magazine*'s "In Harvey Service" column from 1910 to 1912 and are reproduced here just as they were shared and used in Harvey kitchens. Imagine the Harvey House kitchen staff putting together a meal for hungry train passengers with approximately twenty to thirty minutes to eat. Certainly, some things were prepared in advance, but a strict Fred Harvey rule was that the food would be fresh. I suppose the chef knew measurements from experience, and he passed this information on to the staff. A common Harvey Girl story relates the difficulty of dealing with a temperamental chef. In defense of the chef, consider how difficult it would be using the vague instructions of these recipes and cooking for forty-plus diners on a stove fueled with coal. In later years, Harvey recipes were printed on a standard form and distributed to each Harvey House kitchen.

Banana Pie

Peel and slice the bananas thin, add sugar, a little butter and some spice, allspice or a dash of ginger, a little acid syrup, lemon or orange juice. Bake with full cover or put on a meringue when done. Another way is to make a syrup with one-half pint of water and vinegar, one pound of sugar and some allspice, and season the bananas with the syrup.

Beef Rissoles

Cold cooked beef, minced, three parts, and grated bread crumbs, one part; mix and season with herbs, grated rind of lemon, salt and pepper, bound with raw yolks of eggs, made into the shape of an egg, breaded and fried. Serve with a mound of mashed potatoes in the center of the dish, a rissole at each end and side, with some thickened roast beef gravy poured around. Garnish potatoes with parsley. This dish may also be served with kidney beans, green peas, French string beans or mixed vegetables instead of the potatoes.

Bell Pepper (Fred Harvey Style)

Six skinned bell peppers (enough to make twelve orders); two to three onions; three ounces of butter or olive oil; one green pepper; a tablespoon of flour; one crushed clove of garlic; three or four eggplants; two whole eggs; one half-pint of milk; a handful of fresh bread crumbs. Remove the skin from the peppers by dipping them into hot grease. Peel the eggplant and cut in dice a quarter of an inch thick. Cut the peppers in two lengthwise, remove the fleshy part adhering to the seeds, chop it and add to the eggplant. Cut the onions and green peppers fine; put on the fire with oil or butter and let cook for ten minutes. Add the crumbs, garlic, eggplant, a little salt and stir frequently until done. Add the flour; mix well; pour in the milk; let come to a boil and keep stirring. Add the eggs and a little chopped parsley. Mix well, season if necessary and remove from the fire. Stuff the bell peppers with this mixture. Sprinkle with grated cheese; put a small lump of butter on each one and leave them in a hot oven long enough to produce a nice golden brown.

Chestnut Pudding

Peel and boil three pints of chestnuts until tender, remove the skins and press through a sieve. Mix with one-half pound of butter, three-quarters of a pound of sugar, two cups of sweet milk and four well-beaten eggs. Flavor with vanilla. Beat well together, pour into a buttered pudding mold, cover tightly and steam for one hour. Serve very hot with orange syrup and sections of candied orange.

Chicken a la King

Take the breasts of tender fowls, slice in size desired. Let simmer in fresh butter a while. Add for one fowl two gills (one-half pint) of sherry wine; one small cupful of cream. Season to taste. Beat together four yolks of eggs and a quarter cupful of cream. Parboil and dice one green pepper, one sweet pepper; slice four mushrooms. Mix all ingredients together.

Clam Soup

One heaping tablespoon of butter and two of flour, rubbed into a cream. Melt in a saucepan over the fire and add slowly a quart of rich milk, stirring constantly; when it thickens add celery salt, a bit of cayenne and a cup of minced clams with their juice; let it come to a boil and serve.

Cocoanut [sic] Bars

Five whites of eggs beaten very stiff; add ten ounces of granulated sugar, seven ounces of cocoanut (*sic*); mix together, spread on wafer paper and cut in finger shapes. Place on buttered pans and bake in a cool oven.

Cranberry Sherbet

Place one quart of cranberries in three cups of boiling water and let boil about ten minutes. When the berries are well softened, strain through a sieve. Let one and one-half cupsful of sugar, in one quart of water, boil twenty minutes. Add one tablespoonful of gelatin that has been soaked in two tablespoons of cold water. When cool, strain and add the cranberries, with more sugar if desired. Then freeze as usual.

Dandelion Salad

Wash, pick over, and cook dandelions until tender in boiling water to which has been added one-eighth teaspoonful soda. Add together one Neufchatel cheese, four hard boiled eggs, three-quarters of a cup of cooked dandelions,

Right: The cover of a 1940 Bright Angel Lodge breakfast menu. *Courtesy of Tom Taylor.*

Below: A variety of breakfast items were offered at Bright Angel Lodge, including filet of sole and sautéed calf's liver with bacon along with traditional pancakes, ham and eggs. *Courtesy of Tom Taylor.*

Club Breakfasts

ITEMS PRICED DETERMINE COST OF BREAKFAST
Served from 6:00 a. m. to 11:30 a. m.

CHOICE OF FRUIT OR CEREAL

Baked Apple		Half Grapefruit
Pineapple Slice	Stewed Prunes, with Cream	Apple Sauce
Figs in Syrup	Orange Juice Grapefruit Juice	Tomato Juice
Oatmeal	Grape Nuts	Puffed Wheat
Cream of Wheat	Corn Flakes All Bran	Bran Flakes
	Served with Cream	

Filet of Sole, Saute, Potatoes	65
Boiled Salt Mackerel, Steamed Potato	65
Two Eggs, Boiled or Fried 50; Poached 55; on Toast	60
Omelette, with Minced Ham	65
Little Pig's Sausages or Sausage Cakes	75
Wheat Cakes 55; with Ham, Bacon or Sausages	70
Buck Wheat Cakes 55; with Ham, Bacon or Sausages	70
French Toast, with Currant Jelly	65
Fried Corn Meal Mush, with Bacon and Maple Syrup	65
Ham or Bacon, with 1) Egg 50; with (2) Eggs	60
Chipped Beef in Cream on Toast	60
Corned Beef Hash, Plain 55; with Fried Egg	60
Calf's Liver, Saute, with Bacon	75
Broiled French Lamb Chops (2) au Cresson	85
Pork Chops, (2) Saute, with Apple Sauce	80
Sweet Roll or Toast and Jelly	40

Rolls	Toast		Muffins
Iced Tea or Coffee	Coffee Tea	Cocoa	Milk

Breakfast a la Carte

FRUITS

Baked Apple 15; with Cream 20		Half Grapefruit 10
Sliced Orange 10; whole 05		Sliced Pineapple 20
Stewed Prunes 15; with Cream 20		Apple Sauce 15
Figs in Syrup 20 Orange Juice 10		Tomato Juice 10
Grapefruit Juice 10		Pineapple Juice 10

CEREALS

Oatmeal Puffed Wheat	Grape Nuts	Bran
Cream of Wheat Corn Flakes	Shredded Wheat	
Served With Cream 25		

SPECIAL DISHES

Wheat Cakes, with Ham, Bacon or Sausages	60
Buck Wheat Cakes, with Ham, Bacon or Sausages	60
Ham or Bacon, with Eggs 50; half portion 35	
Chipped Beef in Cream on Toast	50
Broiled Ham or Bacon 55; Half Portion 35	
Broiled French Lamb Chops	75
Corned Beef Hash, Plain 50; with Egg 55	
Calf's Liver and Bacon 65	
French Toast, with Currant Jelly	45

EGGS

Two Eggs—Boiled, Fried or Scrambled, with Potatoes	30
Poached Eggs, Plain 35; on Toast 40	
Omelettes, with Minced Ham or Bacon 50; plain	40

POTATOES

American Fried 15	Hashed Browned 15	Creamed 20

ROLLS, DOUGHNUTS, HOT CAKES, TOAST;

Small or Twist 10	Dry or Buttered Toast 10	Hot Rolls 10
Doughnuts 10	Bread 05	Wheat Cakes 30
Melba Toast 10		Cinnamon Toast 15

PRESERVES

Strained Honey 15 Orange Marmalade 15 Currant Jelly 15

BEVERAGES

Coffee 10	Tea, per Pot 15	Cocoa, per Pot 20
Bottle Milk 10	Kaffee Hag 15 Postum 15	Buttermilk 10
Iced Tea or Coffee, per Glass 10		

SACCHARINE MAY BE HAD FROM YOUR WAITRESS ARRANGEMENTS GLADLY MADE FOR SPECIAL DIET.
IN ADDITION TO PRICES LISTED 1% WILL BE COLLECTED FOR THE STATE SALES TAX
NOT RESPONSIBLE FOR LOSS OF WEARING APPAREL OR PERSONAL EFFECTS 1-19-40

FOR INFORMATION REGARDING SIGHT-SEEING TRIPS, SEE OTHER SIDE olive oil, one-quarter teaspoon of salt, one-eighth teaspoon of cayenne. Rub through a strainer, add the egg yolks and the dandelions separately; add oil until of a consistency to handle; salt and cayenne. Mix thoroughly and, when well blended, shape into balls. Serve on white leaves of lettuce, with French mayonnaise or boiled dressing.

Eggs en Fromage

Beat six eggs very slightly. Place in a chafing dish a tablespoon of butter, and when this is hot throw into two heaping tablespoons of finely grated hard cheese. Stir about until smoothly creamed in the butter, then add the eggs, season with paprika and a little salt, and cook until the eggs are slightly scrambled. Serve on toast.

English Plum Pudding

One pound of suet, chopped fine; two dozen crackers, rolled fine; one pound of raisins; one pound of currants; six eggs; one nutmeg; one cup of sugar; a little salt. Sift a little flour over the mixture—just enough to keep it together. Tie in a cloth, allowing space in which to swell, and boil constantly about five hours. Then turn out onto a platter. Serve hot or cold. Use any preferred sauce.

French Apple Pie with Nutmeg Sauce

Eight cups sliced, tart apples; one-half cup water; one and one-half cups sugar; one recipe plain pastry; one cup all-purpose flour; one-half cup sugar; one-third cup butter; one cup graham crackers crushed; few drops of vanilla. For sauce mix one egg yolk; one-half cup sugar; one cup milk. Het to the boiling point; remove from heat and add nutmeg. Cook apples in water until tender; add sugar and mix carefully to retain shape of apples. Arrange apples in pastry lined pie plate. Combine graham cracker crumbs, flour, sugar, butter and vanilla. Mix until it resembles coarse crumbs, sprinkle mixture over apples. Bake in hot oven ten minutes, then in moderate oven twenty minutes. Serve with Nutmeg Sauce.

The present-day restaurant at La Posada is named the Turquoise Room and located in the area where customers were served in earlier days. *Courtesy of Kathy Weir.*

Fried Green Tomatoes

Cut into thin slices some large, perfectly green specimens (they must not have begun to show any sign of ripening, and those freshly pulled are really best for this dish). Sprinkle with salt and dip in cornmeal until covered. Fry in a little butter until a nice brown. Cover the frying pan throughout the cooking process to keep the tomatoes tender. Serve either plain or with a brown sauce.

German Potato Salad

Boil twelve potatoes. While hot cut in thin slices, cover with finely sliced onions and add one teaspoonful of salt and one half-teaspoonful of pepper. Mix the yolk of one egg with three tablespoonsful of olive oil and four tablespoonsful of vinegar. Pour the well-mixed dressing over the potatoes, then pour a half-cupful of boiling water or broth over the whole mixture and stir well. Sprinkle with chopped parsley; cover and let stand for a few hours. This salad never will be dry.

Lamb Chops a la Nelson

Make a dressing of boiled onions and grated cheese, passing through a sieve; broil chop on one side only, cover the unbroiled side with dressing and place in hot oven to brown; garnish with tongue tips and mushroom tops.

Macaroni and Oysters

Cook macaroni in salted water, without breaking it, till it is soft. Butter a covered mold or small pail quite thickly, and, beginning in the center of the bottom, coil the macaroni around. As it begins to rise on the sides put in a layer of oysters, only half cooked, mixed with a thick cream sauce, and then add more macaroni, and so on until the mold is full. Put on the cover and cook in a kettle of boiling water for half an hour. Turn out on a hot platter and surround with cheese balls made by adding melted butter and chopped parsley to grated American cheese and molding into shape. Pass a bowl of cream sauce with this.

Mackerel Baked in Cream

Skin, bone and divide a large fish into four pieces, season and fry in butter, drain it and put the pan where it will keep hot. Mix half a pint of white stock, or Bechamel sauce, with the yolk of an egg, stir over the fire for a minute or two, pour over the fish and put chopped parsley and onions and breadcrumbs over the top of the fish.

Meat Pie, Potato Crust

Cut cold roast beef in thin slices, removing all fat and gristle. Cover the bones and trimmings with cold water; add a few slices of onions and carrots, also a stalk of celery. Let simmer two hours. Strain off the broth and simmer

EL TOVAR

GRAND CANYON
NATIONAL PARK
ARIZONA

Right: The cover of a 1939 El Tovar menu reflects the more formal nature of the hotel restaurant. *Courtesy of Tom Taylor.*

Below: Menu choices at El Tovar in 1939. The choices on the right are included in the one-dollar dinner price. *Courtesy of Tom Taylor.*

A LA CARTE MENU

FRUITS, ETC.
Half Grapefruit 15   Stewed Rhubarb 20   Grapefruit Juice 15
Orange Juice 15   Tomato Juice 15   Sauerkraut Juice 15
Stewed Prunes 20   Sliced Fresh Pineapple 20   Apple Sauce 20
Sliced Banana, with Cream 25   Half Cantaloupe 20
Fresh Figs, with Cream 30   Honey Dew Melon 20
Sliced Fresh Peaches, with Cream 30

CEREALS, WITH CREAM
Shredded Wheat 25   Cream of Wheat 25   Rolled Oats 25
Corn Flakes 25   Puffed Rice 25   Grape Nuts 25
All-Bran 25   Bran Flakes 25

FISH
Steamed Salt Mackerel, Drawn Butter 65   Clam Bouillon 25
Grilled Filet of Barracuda, Butter Sauce 65

MEATS, ETC.
Ham 60   Bacon 60; with Eggs 65   Half Portion 45
Chipped Beef in Cream 55
French Toast, with Currant Jelly 60
Broiled Lamb Chops 75
Calf's Liver and Bacon 65
Browned Corned Beef Hash, with Poached Eggs 60
Hot Cakes, with Ham or Bacon 60

EGGS
Eggs (2) Boiled, Fried or Scrambled 35   Plain Omelette 50
Poached Eggs on Toast 40   Spanish Omelette 65

POTATOES
Saute Potatoes 20

HOT CAKES
Wheat Cakes, with Maple Syrup 35

DOUGHNUTS, ETC.
Snails 15   Doughnuts 15

ROLLS, ETC.
Hot Rolls 10   Corn Muffins 10   Toast 15

PRESERVES
Honey 20   Orange Marmalade 20   Currant Jelly 20

COFFEE, ETC.
Tea 20   Coffee per pot 25; per cup 15   Cocoa 20   Milk 15

Breakfast 7 to 9   Luncheon 12 to 2   Dinner 6 to 8

TABLE D'HOTE BREAKFAST
$1.00

Grapefruit   Fresh Stewed Rhubarb   Grapefruit Juice
Orange Juice   Tomato Juice   Sauerkraut Juice
Stewed Prunes   Sliced Fresh Pineapple   Apple Sauce
Half Cantaloupe   Sliced Banana   Honey Dew Melon
Fresh Figs   Sliced Fresh Peaches

Cream of Wheat   Rolled Oats   Shredded Wheat   Bran Flakes
Puffed Rice   Corn Flakes   Puffed Rice
Grape Nuts   All-Bran

Clam Bouillon

Steamed Salt Mackerel, Drawn Butter
Grilled Filet of Barracuda, Butter Sauce

Fried Hominy Grit, with Maple Syrup and Bacon
Corn Fritters, with Syrup and Rasher of Bacon
Chipped Beef in Cream
French Toast, with Currant Jelly
Broiled Lamb Chops or Veal Chop
Calf's Liver and Bacon
Browned Corned Beef Hash, with Poached Egg
Ham   Bacon

Eggs as Ordered
Jelly, Creole, Cheese or Parsley Omelette

Saute Potatoes

Wheat Cakes, with Maple Syrup

Hot Rolls   Corn Muffins   Toast
Honey   Orange Marmalade   Currant Jelly
Tea   Coffee   Cocoa   Milk

Monday, July 24, 1939

ARRANGEMENTS GLADLY MADE FOR SPECIAL DIET.
NOT RESPONSIBLE FOR LOSS OF WEARING APPAREL OR PERSONAL EFFECTS

FOR INFORMATION REGARDING SIGHT-SEEING TRIPS, SEE OTHER SIDE in it the slices of beef until they are tender. Season with salt and pepper and sprinkle with flour. Cover with a potato crust, leaving an opening at the top. Bake for fifteen minutes.

Rice Pudding

Wash and boil two tablespoonsful of rice in water to cover. Dissolve a quarter of a boxful of gelatin in cold water and stir into the rice while hot. Allow this to cool, then add a cupful of sugar, two tablespoonsful of chopped, preserved figs. Put on ice several hours. Serve with whipped cream.

Scrapple

One pound of sausage meat; one tablespoon of salt; four quarts of cold water; one pound of cornmeal. The sausage should be mixed first with a small quantity of water until the particles are separated, then the mixture should be boiled hard before adding the meal, very slowly at first, stirring continually with a wooden spoon or ladle. Add the meal as in making mush, never allowing it to stop boiling, and when it is the consistency of a stiff batter, turn it into moistened pans until the next morning. It should be sliced and then fried crisp in hot fat and served.

Swedish Meat Balls

One pound of lean pork shoulder; eight small toasts; three boiled potatoes; one onion. Put all ingredients through a grinder, emptying into a bowl. Then add two eggs, and salt and pepper to taste. Work together thoroughly and make them into balls, then fry.

Tomato and Green Pepper Salad

Cut rather thick slices of peeled tomatoes and spread each with finely chopped green pepper, mixed with French dressing; on each one put three very tiny white onions, cooked and peeled, with French dressing over all.

French Dressing

Tarragon vinegar, one part; olive oil, four parts; paprika, salt and pepper. Mix very thoroughly, having a piece of ice in the bowl. [Note: although Fred Harvey would not sanction the use of anything but olive oil of the very highest grade, those to whom the flavor of olive oil is distasteful will find peanut oil an excellent substitute. It is much less expensive and cuts the vinegar equally as well, producing a most palatable dressing.]

PRACTICAL HARVEY KITCHEN TIPS

> To preserve the natural sweetness, color and flavor of green peas, cook them in their shells. Put them in a steamer until they are done. It will take two-thirds less time to shell them than when raw, and they will require but very little seasoning.

> Corn on the cob is cooked to perfection by putting it in a steamer, dry, for twenty minutes with a moderate steam. Then dip the ears into a pan containing hot water, milk and salt, and they will be ready to serve.

> Potatoes baked in their skins always will come out more dry and mealy if a small piece is cut off one end to allow the steam to escape in the cooking.

> Green vegetables should be boiled fast, with a pinch of carbonate of soda, with the sauce-pan lid off.

> Jelly should not be put into the mold until it is on the point of setting. If this rule is observed there never will be any difficulty in turning out the most delicate cream, jelly or aspic.

SELECTED BIBLIOGRAPHY

Bell, James B. *Ghost Trains: Images from America's Railroad Heritage*. New York: Chartwell Books, 2014.

Dugan, Brenna Stewart. "Girls Wanted: For Service at the Fred Harvey Houses." Graduate thesis, Texas Tech University, December 2008.

Foster, George H., and Peter C. Weiglin. *The Harvey House Cookbook: Memories of Dining along the Santa Fe Railroad*. Atlanta: Longstreet Press, 1992.

Grattan, Virginia L. *Mary Colter: Builder upon the Red Earth*. Flagstaff, AZ: Northland Press, 1980.

Henderson, James D. *Meals by Fred Harvey: A Phenomenon of the American West*. Fort Worth: Texas Christian University Press, 1969.

Howard, Kathleen L., and Diana F. Pardue. *Inventing the Southwest: The Fred Harvey Company and Native American Art*. Flagstaff, AZ: Northland Publishing, 1998.

Latimer, Rosa Walston. *Harvey Houses of Kansas: Historic Hospitality from Topeka to Syracuse*. Charleston, SC: The History Press, 2015.

———. *Harvey Houses of New Mexico: Historic Hospitality from Raton to Deming*. Charleston, SC: The History Press, 2015.

———. *Harvey Houses of Texas: Historic Hospitality from the Gulf Coast to the Panhandle*. Charleston, SC: The History Press, 2014.

Lutzick, Ann-Mary J., Winslow Historical Society and the Old Trails Museum Archives. *Winslow*. Charleston, SC: Arcadia Publishing, 2013.

Marshall, James. *Santa Fe: The Railroad That Built an Empire*. New York: Random House, 1945.

Melzer, Richard. *Fred Harvey Houses of the Southwest.* Charleston, SC: Arcadia Publishing, 2008.

Poling-Kempes, Lesley. *The Harvey Girls: Women Who Opened the West.* New York: Paragon House, 1989.

Thomas, Diane. *The Southwestern Indian Detours.* Phoenix, AZ: Hunter Publishing, 2002.

INDEX

ABOUT THE AUTHOR

Photograph by Rockin' W Photography.

Rosa Walston Latimer, who lives in Austin, Texas, is an author, playwright and an award-winning photographer. She writes for national and regional magazines and was news editor of a print and an online newspaper and supervising director of a nationally syndicated television program. Rosa is also a writing consultant and conducts workshops on writing nonfiction and memoir.

The story of her Harvey Girl grandmother sparked Rosa's interest in preserving women's history. After being told by a museum curator in another state that there were no Harvey Houses in Texas, Rosa was determined to preserve this important part of the state's railroad history and inspired to write her first book, *Harvey Houses of Texas: Historic Hospitality from the Gulf Coast to the Panhandle*. The author has now chronicled her grandmother's story, as well as the stories of many other New Mexico Harvey Girls, in her second book, *Harvey Houses of New Mexico: Historic Hospitality from Raton to Deming*. While working on these books, Rosa realized the Kansas Harvey House story should be told—after all, Kansas is where the Harvey House story began! Her third book, *Harvey Houses of Kansas: Historic Hospitality from Topeka to Syracuse*, was published in 2015 and selected by the Kansas Center for the Book, a program of the Kansas State Library, as a "Kansas

Notable Book" in 2016. The exciting story of the Fred Harvey legacy making its way across Arizona—with an impressive presence at the Grand Canyon—was the inspiration for this fourth book in the Harvey House series.

Visit us at
www.historypress.com